Man and Wife

THE PHYSICAL AND
SPIRITUAL FOUNDATIONS
OF MARRIAGE

Rev. Marc Oraison

Translated from the French by
Andre Humbert

NEW YORK : THE MACMILLAN COMPANY

NIHIL OBSTAT:
Martinus S. Rushford, Ph.D.
Censor librorum

IMPRIMATUR:
✠ Bryan Josephus McEntegart
Episcopus Bruklyniensis

BRUKLYNI
Die xii decembris, 1957.

Introduction

THE CURRENT flood of publications, articles and books dealing with marital questions is clearly indicative of the degree to which such problems have impinged on the modern conscience. Though it might be supposed that an increased freedom of expression in the matter of psycho-sexual realities has given impetus to this study, there are deeper reasons for its being the order of the day.

The first of these is an awakening to consciousness, at the behest of the Magisterium of the Church, concerning the moral importance of sex and its practices. It seems quite clear indeed that Christians at the end of the nineteenth century and the beginning of the twentieth century had more or less lost sight of this significant part of human life. Under the guise of good breeding or of modesty the thinking of that time avoided facing up to certain issues, and therefore fell short of sufficient reflection upon them. Errors of judgment, frequently quite grave, had become verities whose wording took such forms as, "youth must have its fling," or "a man must sow his wild oats before settling down in marriage." At the same time marital and social relations were more or less avowedly conditioned by a particular view of womanhood against which Mme. Simone de Beauvoir has every right to raise her voice, though she has done it poorly. This concept of womanhood is reflected in the literature and the theatre of the era, as shown in Anouilh's *Ardèle or the Daisy*. Even Christian conscience, by dint of sexual modesty, came to be uninformed about the most elementary truths. When the clear, exhaustive and indisputable teachings of Pius XI in the Encyclical *Casti connubii* focused their light upon these shadowy regions, there necessarily resulted much confusion, some dismay, but at least universal consideration.

Another reason for the widespread interest in sex and marital problems stems from facts of a social nature. The great lowering of incidence of infant mortality attributable to the remarkable advances in medical techniques necessarily raises the question of the increase and distribution of the world population, not alone on the national or the world-wide scale, but even on the plane of the family itself. The erstwhile and cruel process of selection which operated by means of communicable and toxic diseases, of unrelented hereditary ailments, now is on the way to being a thing completely of the past. Quite abruptly, then, looms the problem not of "limiting" births, but rather of "regulating" the population of the family, according to the felicitous expression of Pope Pius XII. The equilibrium of the family group as well as the very future of the children may be in question as never before. The normal consequence of such a development is the sharp and utterly in-escapable question, "Does the regulation of births involve the Christian conscience in the problem of having to regulate sex?" Put thus, it seems like a truism, for certainly morals have always been taught. But the point here is that we are *now* taken up with the practical importance of this actual moral option, and with all the problems of knowledge and action which it raises. Stirred by the suddenness of such a summons, our modern times can be an age of profound study and privileged training in all the aspects of the mystery of sex and its meaning. And further-more since sexuality—as is made clearer every day—is bound up with what is deepest in man's psychology as much as with what is most mysterious in his creative dynamism, it will be no surprise if the modern age shall be a time of avid search, of controversy, of progress and error admixed.

However, the problem of behavior in married life is still too often badly presented. It would seem that between the universal and sovereign teaching of the Church, on the one hand, and the disposition of the faithful to receive it, on the other, there should be a closer drawing together, a deepening of thought and a greater explicitness in understanding. Because there is some lagging on these points the present current of thought tends to envisage marital behavior as a legalistic issue rather than a moral one. This surely is the easy solution, but one which too often distorts the true meaning of Christian doctrine and succeeds only in discouraging the faithful who feel that their difficulties are met with cold misunderstanding. In fact, as one talks over these problems with married couples for whom Christian belief is a matter of utmost concern, it soon becomes apparent that while they know the Law in its blunt dictates, they are woefully ignorant of many of the biological, psychological, and even the theological data which that very Law takes for granted as it makes its dynamic pronouncements. In other words, the faithful know full well the precepts, but they know nothing of the foundation underlying the precepts, nor do they realize how the precepts constitute a varied and cohesive whole which might be called the vital rhythm of man on his way toward his destiny.

We lay no claims in the following pages to an exhaustive study of this very complex problem. It is our intention merely to attempt an outline or a broad survey that will help to make explicit the Christian teaching on marriage, and thus help married people and those who will be married toward a better understanding of that doctrine.

Contents

1
Sex and the Sexual Instinct
in General Biology

To WHATEVER heights we rise in reflecting on matters of a spiritual or mystical order, we should never lose touch with the concrete reality in which such considerations are grounded. Nor should our perception of the lofty character of man's vocation, through divine grace, to eternal life cause us to forget that man must reach that destiny just as he is; and that it is impossible for him to begin thinking of his goal, or to prepare for it adequately without taking account of the complex reality of human nature.

Preliminary physiological considerations

Man, by his physical nature, is in unbroken continuity with the universe of living and particularly animal creatures. The characteristic trait of such a world is the organization of matter into independent organisms characterized by growth and interchange. Thus, life is seen to be divided into functions; and the first fact about all living beings as such, including man, is that they belong to a physiological order. Before proceeding to any speculation about our subject, it would therefore seem to be essential to examine the nature of the sexual function common to all living beings above a certain level in the scale of creatures and specifically under the aspect of its physiological organization and significance. For all the spirituality which is specific to him, man must necessarily reconcile himself to this fact; for the first law which is imposed upon him is that of his physiological structure. This is a point which, in our opinion, is too often passed over in silence or even disavowed. Either attitude is highly prejudicial to a correct understanding of the issues involved.

1. Certain physiological organs are grouped into an aggregate whose bond is the interdependence of one organ upon the other, and whose purpose is the exercise of some particular activity of the living being. This aggregate of organs is called a system, and the activating, dynamic and vital element insuring the function of the system is called an instinct. Thus in regard to the components of sexuality, the anatomy of the living organism is designed by nature for reproduction; and the sexual instinct impels the individual to play his part in reproduction within a particular species.

The endocrine mechanism releases in the female the production of certain cellular elements which contain half of the specific corpuscles of the species under consideration. Simultaneously, and by another phase of the same process, the organ of gestation is so prepared as to enable the fruit of fecundation to live through the first period of its existence in conditions most favorable to its development. In the male, there occurs the production of complementary cellular elements as well as the preparation of such conditions as will be necessary so that the semen shall be deposited at a time and in the place and manner most favorable for fecundation. The physical union of the sexes is totally designed, in its physiological reality, for the meeting and the fusion of the complementary cellular elements in such a way that one or more living individuals of the species shall be brought into existence and shall develop. From the physiological point of view there is absolutely no other reason for the existence of the sexual function. Of course the normal exercise of this function tends to bring about both in the male and the female a certain pleasurable fulfillment of each one's proper and specific sexuality. But this fulfillment must be viewed as a consequence, and not as the goal of the sexual function. For just as the digestive apparatus insures the processes of assimilation, growth and sustenance, the sexual function directly insures reproduction. The ways in which these two functions operate are, of course, radically different; but it remains true that both of them are directed toward insuring one result. It cannot be too often emphasized that sexuality in the living world has for its specific role the reproduction of the species. And anyone who does not, in his reflections on this subject, set out from this elementary fact or does not take it into strict account would run the serious risk of losing touch with the most fundamental data on the matter.

The instinct which insures in the individual the

exercise of the sexual function is necessarily in direct relationship with the role of the function. This instinct, a vital force, impels individuals of complementary sex to unite bodily in such a way that in accordance with very diverse anatomical structures fecundation may take place under conditions naturally required for the perpetuation and extension of the species. It is possible that this extension of the species may encounter obstacles which may at times be insurmountable. Or it may happen that the energies which make for fecundity spend themselves in vain, and that a species once known to history may disappear from the living world despite normal exercise of the sexual function in its individual representatives. This does not alter the fact that the instinct or driving force which insures the exercise of the sexual function is oriented, of itself, to procreation. This is a primary biological datum universally applicable, and it must serve as our basic certitude in this investigation.

2. But there exists a radical difference between the sexual function and the other functions in the physiology of the living individual, and consequently between the sexual instinct and the other instincts. Sensory perceptions and other activities like digestion, assimilation, excretion, as well as the various mechanisms of defense—all these are directed to maintaining the individual in his existence and proper balance. The instincts which forcefully activate these particular functions have in some way their origin and goal in the individual himself. Apparently, each of the individual "wholes" we know as separate living beings is endowed with sources of autonomous energy which enable it to assure life,

to defend it, and to extend its range of influence. Thus if one of these instincts should fail in one of these living beings, the very life of the individual would be threatened, either at its root or in one of its essential modes of action. And it is this particular living individual, and he alone, who would suffer directly through an impairment of that balance of forces which makes him what he is.

Now the sexual instinct, insuring as it does a function that transcends the individual, cannot have him as its final goal, even though it originates in him. The sex instinct was not designed by nature to insure the existence of the individual who possesses it but rather to insure the existence of a much larger reality, one in which the individual stands as a component element. It corresponds to a vital need of the species, and the individual can contribute to the species only inasmuch as he can do no more than participate singly in that vital need of the species. In a sense the sexual function is, as it were, a superabundant activity in the individual, for it cannot be exercised until the individual has attained a certain level of development and power; and, moreover, its exercise by the individual is not a requirement for his self-perpetuation. To risk a comparison, the sexual instinct may be regarded as similar to the "musical instinct" of a member of an orchestra who is moved by it to share in the creation of music through collaboration with others, and thus to bring about something which transcends him and, even while it requires his personal presence, is not directed to his own being or to maintaining him in his particular existence.

3. From all this there results a very important

practical consequence with regard to the sexual function. If, for serious reasons, an individual cannot exercise his sexual activity according to the way nature has disposed this function in him, then it is possible for him to suspend this activity without going contrary to any of the essential intentions of nature's plan. For nature requires certain modes of action in the harmonious unfolding of the sexual activities, but does not imperatively demand that the sex function be exercised. Other human instincts are a matter of nature's command: one may say in a sense that the individual cannot possibly refuse to obey them, and therefore does not have the right, physiologically speaking, to suspend their exercise. Refusal to respond to their commands would endanger existence itself, whereas suspending the exercise of his own sexual function constitutes nothing more than a refusal to participate in the continuation and extension of the species.

The decisive question here is only to know whether the motives which make the individual withdraw from collaboration with the species are of sufficient importance, or to determine whether the individual is simply shirking his responsibilities in this regard. A valid motive for failure to share in the extension of the species would, of course, be isolation from members of the complementary sex. And there can also be other legitimate reasons: the instinct of self-preservation in the female can sometimes require temporary or definitive suspension of the sexual function when its exercise has become dangerous for her. Furthermore it may be to the interest of the species to demand that no progeny be brought forth which might disturb the balance of the species, impair its worth and curtail its potentialities for existence or expansion.

We have deliberately chosen to dwell for the moment on the level of very general considerations in order to point out that the basic meaning of sexuality in the living being is a universal one, regardless of the manner in which particular individuals, animal or human, put this power to use.

Moreover, experience has established that an individual who refrains from all sexual activity suffers no harm to life or health. It is quite clear that the sexual instinct, corresponding as it does to the sexual function, implies for the individual a need to exercise it; but it cannot be called, in the strict sense, a vital need. Even if real difficulties sometimes arise from the frustration of the sexual need, these are essentially transitory and superficial matters, at least from the viewpoint of biological balance. Such frustrations can accurately be described as painful, but will not, however prolonged they may be, have any repercussions on the individual's essential traits.

In the animal races it is generally the female who suffers the most from sexual frustration. The behavior pattern of a female cat or dog which is isolated during its period of heat reveals that for several days the animal suffers discomfort, agitation and fretfulness. However, this is a matter of biological alternation, and once it is over, everything returns to normalcy until the next troublesome period occurs. At no time is the animal's health or life in jeopardy. And the male animal isolated from the female in the period of heat does not manifest any great symptoms of discomfort, nor is its health in any way threatened. It is hardly necessary to stress further the radical difference which in this respect distinguishes the sexual instinct from the other instincts, directed as these latter are to the maintenance and the defense of the individual's actual existence.

From another point of view one may also state that the setting in motion of the physiological sex function differs fundamentally from that of other biological functions. The source of energy needed to activate the latter lies essentially in a definite physiological condition of the organism which demands, under pain of death, that a given change take place within a rather short interval of time. Hunger and thirst, for example, indicate an organic deficiency which cannot be allowed to continue for long, while excretive needs express the absolute necessity of ejecting from the living body the waste products whose toxicity is a direct threat to life. Nothing of the sort obtains where the sexual instinct is concerned. In the female the ovarian cycle periodically calls for the setting in motion of the sexual process, but not in any absolute or unconditional way. In the male, where the sexual function is always virtually possible, it is aroused only through certain sensory perceptions which set reflexes in motion; but even then there is no absolute demand on the part of his organism; for the genital apparatus does not function in the same way as the stomach, the intestines or the bladder. Therefore, when someone talks of sexual "hunger" or "thirst," or of man's need "to void a certain fullness" of sexual nature, such language constitutes an analogy in a most unacceptable sense, tending as it does to sanction a deep-seated confusion and a fundamental error with regard to the physiology of sex.

At this point it may be objected that what we have stated so far is a very odd beginning for a book with pretensions to a discussion of conjugal morality. Our answer is that no aspect of man should be ignored; and since man has been defined in classical terms as a "rational animal," it becomes necessary to acquire the clearest possible knowledge of the way this "animal" lives. Once such knowledge has been secured, it is easier to discover how the "rational" element in him can take over control of this vital activity and invest it with human meaningfulness. It is therefore important, we believe, to underscore the fact that sexual continence is, physiologically speaking, completely legitimate, possible, and in no way harmful to the fundamental balance of the living organism.

4. When some activity is practiced counter to the norms of nature, harmful consequences are not long in catching up with the individual involved, for nature has a way of imposing sanctions on those who flout her laws. Once again, however, there are considerable differences where the so-called instinct of preservation and the sexual instinct are concerned.

It is only logical that it should be so. The instinct to eat, for example, is directed to the preservation of individual life; and it is the individual himself who will be endangered if the instinct is exercised in a fashion contrary to its proper laws and to the intentions of nature. The consequences of abuse may be indigestion, or intoxication, or starvation, or still some other condition that jeopardizes immediate personal existence. But if the sexual instinct is exercised in defiance of normal physiological standards or of the end for which it was naturally intended, the sanctions will be pressed not on the individual but on the species, because the function of the sexual instinct is directly oriented to the species itself, as was stated earlier. The species will be wanting in new members, a result which upsets the general balance and the life of the race. This fact will hardly be evident, at first sight, to the observer whose view is limited in time and in space. For the individual or the couple guilty of this biological perversion, repercussions may be so slight as hardly to be noticeable; they may even be physiologically nonexistent, for integrity in the exercise of this function does not affect the individual as an individual, but only to the extent that he is one with the human species. An aberration in regard to diet cannot be sustained for a long time without great damage to life; but sexual abnormality can be habitual without exacting penalties any more serious than abstention from sexual acts.

This last consideration is an important one. Man, however proud he may be about his independence and strength, remains in his daily behavior subject to elemental—and sometimes salutary—fears. Dangerous eccentricities in dietary matters will quickly be tagged by current opinion with the label of useless or disturbing follies. The converse is, however, true in the sphere of sex where the danger is much less apparent, and where sexual aberrations—among which one must from a physiological viewpoint count contraceptive practices, for example, or the systematic indulgence in *amplexus reservatus* *—

---

* *Amplexus reservatus* means intercourse in which penetration takes place and is continued for a time, but in which neither party experiences orgasm before, during, or after the act.

will be looked upon as harmless or even justifiable. People do not see at first glance any harm in such practices because, save for certain exceptional cases, there seems to be no physiological or perceptible damage done to the individual.

Let us say further that man seems to be altogether utilitarian in his basic impulses: he has a strong tendency to consider as good whatever does him no harm, and to view as evil whatever is immediately and obviously injurious to him. Such elementary utilitarianism is insufficient grounding for any true morality. But allowances will always have to be made for that sort of inertia which consists in rising no higher than the level of sensory perceptions, in not wanting to look beyond the tight circle of self, in not taking account of the natural laws when they extend beyond these narrow perspectives, and in not reflecting upon the fate of the species which, for man, encompasses values of transcendent importance. We for our part are quite convinced that such inertia is one of the main obstacles to the formulation of morality in the matters of sex, even for the most cultivated and Christian persons.

It is good then for us to know that an individual may run counter to certain laws of nature without experiencing immediate and serious sanctions. Nevertheless, the individual will really have transgressed the laws of nature. This raises a moral problem of far greater scope and involves values of far greater worth than are found in merely pragmatic considerations.

In spite of the fact that activities contrary to the natural law do not involve personal penalties which are immediate and grave, it is nevertheless true that everything concerned with sex rotates primarily around the pivotal fact of procreation. It is absolutely essential not to forget this fundamental truth which rests not on argumentation but on established facts and clear evidence.

Conclusions

And so, as we are about to discuss conjugal morality, we deem it important to underscore boldly these two biological findings.

First, sexual continence not only is legitimate and feasible, but there are certain circumstances which make it necessary. To be more specific, such dire facts as ill-health, or poverty or inadequate housing may at times demand that the exercise of the procreative function be suspended.

Second, in the face of such conditions as are not of the individual's making, his duties are clear with respect to the natural law: if he wishes to comply with it, he must suspend the sexual function. For if the function is exercised with the deliberate prior and systematic intent of thwarting its ultimate purpose, namely, procreation, the activity then becomes contrary to nature in the strict sense, as would the use of any other organic apparatus for purposes other than those to which it is ordained.

In the eyes of the physiologist and at any level in the scale of living beings, sexuality is primarily and specifically the power to generate life.

2

On Love, the
Foundation of Morality

THE REVOLUTION which Christianity
brought about in human thinking stemmed essentially from its radically novel views upon the world
and upon the world's destiny. Christianity spoke, as
it were, the final word which so far had not been
uttered either by Judaism or by the various pagan
religions. Thereafter, provided only that the boundless vistas of mystery were accepted, all that previously resisted understanding was flooded with light.

Neither the real origins of the human drama nor
the ultimate destiny of the world could be fully
known until Revelation was complete. In the long
period of expectation Judaic thought was still grop-
ing and fumbling about, even with its faith in the
One Transcendent God and its hopes for the Mes-
siah; while pagan thinking, without basic certitudes
necessary even for a starting point, floundered hope-
lessly in more or less puerile anthropomorphic
imaginings. Judaism could not help but confine itself
within a morality which remained legalistic, beset
with fear or too readily tainted with the pharisaic

formalism which later was so vigorously denounced by Christ. Pagan thinkers were at a loss as they mistook deceptive secondary realities for primary and sure values; they even went so far in Greece, for example, as to deify, to a greater or lesser degree, certain human aberrations. This warping of pagan views occurred most clearly in the domain of sex: they gave the freedom of the city to homosexuality, coloring it with touches of poetry and clothing it in a philosophical garb, despite the obvious fact that this aberration is at best an arresting of the sexual instinct at a more or less infantile stage of its development. In short, both Judaic and pagan thought either failed to grasp the exact and definitive meaning of the world and of mankind or completely distorted it.

It is only after Pentecost that everything at last becomes clear. God's slow workings through the course of history have completed their educative task, and now humanity is ready to live out its true adventure.

Henceforth, the entire universe is clearly seen as a coherent and dynamic entity, teeming with matter and with life. It reaches its zenith in man, and man, for the resemblance he bears to the Creator, has been charged with conveying to God the response the universe must give to the divine summons to existence and fulfillment. This reply of man to God is not automatic, compulsory or instinctive; it must be free if it is to attain its true grandeur.

In man, biological functions are intended to be at one and the same time radically identical with those of the animal world, and radically different in their modalities and their significance. What is involved here is no longer the blind obedience of an impersonal universe, but really a dialogue between two free beings: God and Man.

But at the very inception of this dialogue man fumbled his lines, so to speak; he altered the answer he was to give, baffled God's anticipation, and betrayed the expectations of the whole universe. In order that everything may be restored, God must infix Himself within the innermost depths of human nature and reinvigorate the active role of the human free will He Himself had created, taking upon His shoulders even the very consequences of the errors of human free will.

In Christ, then, the dialogue is resumed in the conquest of pride, eventually to result in the supernatural union which is the glorious culmination of the divine plan. From the Canticle of Canticles through the Gospel of St. John and the Apocalypse all Scripture testifies that History, with all its apparent inconsistencies, is the drama of the love between God and His straying creature, Man.

Granting that this drama has recorded a mysterious, original interruption in the advance of created beings toward their destiny, it does not in the least indicate the destruction of human nature in any of its essential traits; it merely reveals the deep wounds and profound disorganization human nature has suffered in the fall. Yet neither is man's mission changed, nor is there any modification of the way in which he must assume the instincts and biological functions of the living creatures in the universe. One thing alone is required: that he agree to resume the dialogue of love with God in close adherence to faith in Christ. As St. Paul puts it:

the era of the Law was allowed to run its course so as to make us aware of the breach between God and us; but the rule of Law dissolved itself completely in the warm light of the era of Grace. And in Scripture the connotations of "Grace" and "Love" are expressed by the same Greek word.

This supreme fulfillment of revelation will, as St. Paul says, guide the formulation of every rule of human conduct. Since we have been saved in Christ, he says in substance, and have been restored to Love, we must live in an entirely new way; and certain things will be seen immediately as inconsistent with our destiny: idolatry, lust in its various forms, theft, avarice, drunkenness, etc., as he explains clearly in his first epistle to the Corinthians (6:9-11). And the complete realization of our destiny must be in the union of ourselves with God, Who is Absolute Love. We can no longer consent to remain as children who understand nothing and confuse all values; we must become adults in the faith (I Cor. 13:11-12). Now this requirement, which we shall examine later in its equivalent on the psychological level, is incompatible with any complacent acceptance of the discord in our instincts brought about as a result of original sin. That is why it seemed essential to St. Paul to explain to the Christians of Corinth that once they were identified with Christ by faith—with all that this implies in the way of a resumption of spiritual progress—they were strictly obliged to acquire a genuinely wholesome estimate of moral values, to live and behave according to their estate as it was finally made clear and definite in Christ.

Morality is no longer merely a question of law,

properly speaking, but it has become above all a question of loving and of consenting to be loved. It is this fundamental force, this participation by nature and by grace in the very essence of God Himself, which is destined from now on to integrate and vivify in the Christian even the most mysterious and primal biological functions. These functions have not changed, for the plan of nature is immutable; but in man, within the range most peculiar to him, namely, that of a love freely and deliberately chosen or accepted, they are raised to a much higher plane.

It is essential to bear in mind that within the scope of the Christian viewpoint on the world discussion of conjugal morality does not consist simply in a restatement of the terms of the old Law, for this did no more with respect to sexual realities than formulate a practical ethic for use in specific instances. Conjugal morality in Christian terms rests essentially on the knowledge of the religious meaning of sexuality and sexual instincts, and on the recognition of the part they play in God's plan for the universe.

Differences between an instinctual and a personal relationship

A close examination of the way animal behavior is regulated causes one to marvel at the perfect adaptability of animal instinct. Everything unfolds, it seems, according to the plan of an amazingly vast, foresighted and scrupulously careful intelligence which could not possibly be caught off guard. How-

ever, in this regulation of behavior the individual
animal takes no part: or rather, we should say that
it plays out its life in compliance with the score that
governs it, at no time striking the faintest note that
might be unexpected or spontaneous; this animal
performer, if we may be allowed to say so, has no
ear for "grace-notes." Vital activities are governed
by an actuality which encompasses the individual
yet transcends him, for it goes beyond the range of
his self-government. This actuality is instinct—an
automatic and, in a way, a blind force. Experiments
of all kinds have conclusively established that the
individual animal is utterly incapable of acting in
a truly spontaneous and autonomous manner in the
face of circumstances alien to him or disruptive of
the line of conduct set by his particular instincts.
When at times there appears to be some measure
of adaptation or adjustment independent from instinct, closer examination will uncover the decep-
tion, since what appeared to be an adaptation was
really the bringing into play of other seldom-used
instincts which are also not truly self-determined.

It is precisely in the domain of the sexual instinct
that this fact is even more striking. Whatever the
modes of action of the genital function in the different species, the controlling factor is always potential
fecundity in the female or, in other words, the
physiological drive which she feels to perpetuate the
species. In higher animals this is easily observed; in
periods of ovarian activity the female enters into a
state of heat and her organism is subjected to complex modifications destined to provoke in the male
the release and development of a whole set of sexual
reflexes. Everything is determined according to the

biological laws of the particular species in such a way that the period of gestation, and for mammifers the period of nursing as well, can run its course without anything else of a genital nature to distract the female from her procreative work. Outside these periods the sexual instinct is totally quiescent in the male as well as in the female, except in cases of artificial excitation in domestic or captive animals. Literally speaking, it is the rhythm of nature's impulses in the species that regulates the whole process, and the individual animal has nothing else to do than harken, as it were, to this rhythm and follow it.

In man, however, the question is entirely different; and it is only a commonplace to point out that instinct in man, though it is as primal a force as in the animal, is definitely dormant and nearly extinct. As an impelling force it no longer suffices to insure normal functioning of all man's biological activities. It can be arrantly wrong regarding the uses of food, for example, or with respect to the reflexes of defense. In the face of nature's nameless hostility there is no creature more disarmed than man, equipped as he is with only the power of his instincts. Moreover, in man certain other forces may oppose normal impulses and by countering natural law may cause serious trouble, as is proved by drug addiction in its various prevalent forms.

It is, then, a fact that the failure of instinct to regulate biological activities leaves a void to be filled by something different. The difference must be fundamental, as this substituting force must no longer transcend the individual but arise from within him: it is man's own independent power to govern himself which will be expected to regulate his life. Therefore, in the realm of man's activity there are no positive advance indications, as there are for the animal; and man's actions will always be absolutely unforeseeable. In a way we have here a kind of negative reality, for it is essentially a case of nondetermination, and one can hardly ask for a positive definition of freedom in this line of discussion. At best, one may say that man is not driven toward his proper goal by any force which transcends him. He is able to participate not only as one of the species but as a living individual in building, through his own personal independent power, his own being and that of the community of mankind. However, it is also possible for him to strike a pose of antagonism toward nature and, for motives that are his secret affair, to set himself up against her laws in a sort of oddly grandiose attitude not allowed to the animal. Capacity for self-construction, capacity to give consent to the laws of nature or to withhold consent, capacity to make choices in the light of intellect, these are the transcendent new values of this animal who is really not just an animal; these are the specific characteristics which make him the image of God, the preeminently Free Being.

All human biological activities, though remaining substantially the same as they are in the animal, take on an immeasurably greater dimension, participating as they do in the life of the mind, whose task it becomes to take them as they are but to raise them to its own level. If man will only assent to the laws of nature, these laws will have echoes in eternity; but if man rebels and goes counter to them, he puts himself at odds with the plan of God Himself and aggravates his own revolt by dragging all creation with him away from God.

It is in the matters of sexual instinct that the rise in tonal register from animality to humanity is particularly striking. The sexual function is not changed, of course, since it remains fundamentally the function for creating life, according to the biological definition of sexuality. But it now demands to be exercised with much less determinism, subject no longer to the automatic imperatives of the species but directed and governed by the mind.

The law of the human species can find its expression only if the individual takes it upon himself through his personal acknowledgment and his freely willed activity. Each human being is therefore a particular and absolute center of decision, which may not be operative in each concrete act but is at least always implied in the specific characteristics of his nature. According to accepted terms, the human being is no longer an individual, precisely, but a person. This means that the law of the species will not move the particular being like a pawn at its service; each being must accept responsibility for this law, accept or refuse it, reenact in himself the whole history of humanity; in a word, must give his individual assent in this manner to the common destiny to which he is contributing. Each human person, as against the individual animal, thus becomes an original, particular and new "chapter heading," as it were, in human history. The sexual function, then, in man is a matter of relationship between persons and not the mere instinctive coming together of individuals.

As evidenced by a study of nature, the sexual function is eminently the one which requires from the individual a relational attitude. Quite obviously the completely normal exercise of this function postulates that two individuals who are fundamentally different in structure enter into relations with each other to a degree in no way required by any other function of their organisms. The result of these relations will be the advent of one or several new individuals with a relationship of dependency of their own, at least during their early existence, upon the parent individuals.

This relational character of sexuality is the intimately logical consequence of the fact that the function itself is ordained to the species. Nevertheless, even though in the animal world the law commands automatic responses, in man the part played by the self-determination of each individual is, in a sense, of equal importance with the general law which governs the species.

Moreover, at man's level in the scale of beings, every biological activity becomes, in principle, a conscious one, *i.e.*, it implies awareness and admits of reflection upon itself. This element of consciousness will normally be more intense as the particular biological function calls more fully into play the relational aspect of the persons. Sexual tropism, which in the animal attracts the male to the female and vice versa, will involve in man all the resources of psychological consciousness. This attraction, which draws one person to another, becomes, properly speaking, love, which must gather in a sort of hierarchical unity and in a certain "line of march" all the quickening forces: organic, vegetative, psychic, emotional and voluntary. Leading this array must be the mind, in the fullest possible light of knowledge and in the greatest possible freedom from all constraints. Instinct is not in command here, but rather love, with all it brings forth in the spiritual, the psychological, and the physical.

Very often, unfortunately, things do not fall into this pattern. Man's exercise of the sexual life does not, for reasons which we shall examine later, always assume this specifically human aspect; but whatever the factual difficulties observable in daily experiences, this high significance of the sexual function ought to be expressed when man exercises it.

The contractual concept

A contract is a mutual and free pledge between two adult persons who know what they are doing and what is involved in the agreement. In the case of the common sharing of sexuality this contract directly involves the species and the existing phase of the species, namely, society. The contract will therefore be public and be concluded before witnesses. The social character of this contract, one which is essential to it, defines it as a joint adherence to an established institution. And even though the juridical character of marriage is not sufficient to express its whole nature, it is one of its intimate necessities. Now this contract, absolutely unique in its kind, is one that pools for a very long task the maximum of human energies possessed by each contracting party. Thus the physical person, the patrimony, the intellectual, emotional and cultural assets, along with everything else each party can contribute, all these resources are placed by the terms of the contract at the service of a common life in which both parties shall find fulfillment of their respective individual personalities. Sex itself is, of course, also placed in the common pool, and this is what specifies this type of union: the capacity of each partner to contribute to the creation of a new life is put at the disposal of the couple considered as one dynamic unit. Since there are societies where everything but sexuality is shared, the unique character of the completeness of this particular reciprocal giving is followed by certain consequences which are peculiar to it. The first is the fact that marital union is official and social, since the very life of society is bound up with it and society is obliged to sponsor its contract. Outside the marriage contract, the exercise of sex can be nothing but true disorder. A second consequence is that marriage must be indissoluble, for existence itself is here pooled for the common use of the partners not only in its unity and intensity but also for its entire duration. If this were not so, marriage would amount to nothing more than a deceptive allurement. Marriage indeed does not merely give to one person the right to enjoy the body of another sexually, but it establishes the mutual right for them to carry love and friendship to the point of creating one or more new persons whose mere presence demands a stability that cannot possibly be impaired, up to and including the civil status of the contract. It may be said in passing that since the partners in marriage are equal, their contract assumes a character of reciprocity. If their association should fall short of possessing unqualified stability, it would lose the distinctive and specifying feature of being a marriage and become simply a transient partnership. It would then serve merely to give an air of legality to a more or less contrived flirtation characterized by vague sentimentality and by a yearning for independence. Such a desire consists precisely in the unwillingness to give everything of oneself to another throughout the whole course of life.

A third consequence of the fact that marriage involves such a complete pooling of all human assets will be that one person shall enter into the contract with no more than one other person. Clearly, if one of the two parties sets aside a certain preserve for his own amatory or emotional pursuits, he shows no respect for what is of the very essence of the marriage contract, namely, the totality of reciprocal giving. In fact, he deceives his partner and society itself. Certain pagan civilizations, seemingly very primitive as regards material and technical progress, have such a keen perception of this necessity that they punish the adulterer with death, as was done under the Mosaic Law.

But this necessity becomes all the more imperative if one considers sexuality from the point of view of love, an aspect which is much more profound than the merely juridic. To become truly human, *i.e.*, to be in harmony with man's intellect, sexual relations must have perspectives which look forth into the infinite.

In the light of revelation we learn that charity is the only really enduring value, as St. Paul says; for it is, as St. John tells us, real participation in the intimate nature of the Godhead. This love will be fully realized far beyond the limits of created nature in the society of total love in participation with God, which is the kingdom of Heaven. Human destiny has to be considered with regard to this outcome under pain of being wrongly deprived of the ultimate divine gift which fulfills it. The amplitude of the eventual association of man with God infinitely surpasses limited temporal experiences, but nevertheless the achievements of human love in time are a preparation for that eternal and infinite destiny and, as it were, a distant anticipation and reflection of it.

Human love is therefore a privileged experiencing of what charity can be between two persons. For two people, to love is to build something together, both contributing in joint effort all the elements needed to achieve the stated objective. Quite clearly, the reciprocity of giving of two persons in time is strikingly similar, in an essential though a very limited way, to what will take place in eternity. It implies on the part of each person the utmost willingness to give to the other everything, even one's very being, without reservation, once and for all time. For only in this way shall account be taken of the twofold need that marriage be indissoluble and that it stand as the relation of one person to one person.

Marriage is, then, made specifically what it is by the sharing of everything, including sexuality. For this reason it is absolutely necessary not to lose sight of the immutable meaning of its function, which is the fusing of two human persons in their most intimate organisms for the creation of new life. In the Christian view, marriage is a preparation for the kingdom of God, because it not only gives to the two spouses a true realization of the meaning of community in love but contributes to the growth of the Mystical Body, supplying to it members foreseen in the divine plan for the world.

Short of defaulting in his share in the formation of this eternal society, man will be disposed to shape his sexual conduct with the meaning sex has in its relation to the Church. For even though sex is not eternal, as Christ has told us in Luke 20:36, Mark 12:25 and Matthew 22:30, it nevertheless serves to increase the Mystical Body in bringing to it, according to the admirable imagery of the liturgy of Dedication, new "living stones." Not without some astonishment does one reflect on the fact that so momentous a task has been left to the goodwill and free choice of human persons.

In view, then, of the unfolding in time of the human species which is destined to be in eternity the Church Triumphant, two complementary persons will underwrite God's plan and form a community. This community must be made as perfect as possible. Oddly enough, modern psychology offers special confirmation of this point, for Freud, in his study of the sexual instinct, was led to assert that from the purely psychological viewpoint the ideal balance of this instinct in man must reside in a harmonious synthesis of all the emotional and sensory complexes into a spontaneous attitude which is totally directed to the giving of oneself to another person.

Any self-centeredness will therefore be opposed to love from the outset and, as can be definitely stated, will even impede the normal exercise of the psychological instinct of love. This truth, which belongs as much to philosophical reflection as to psychological study, logically requires that the sexual union be indissoluble and exclusive of all but one party if such union is to be perfect. A gift of self which was not permanent, total and exclusive would imply egocentrism and consequently would denote a definite deficiency of love. Inasmuch as it is a question for man to prepare himself in this life for an eternal divine love which is absolutely perfect, he cannot here below give currency to a devaluated concept of human love.

Aside from this consideration there is also need to reflect on the person who results from the sharing of the sexual function in marriage: the child. Common sense alone should dictate that two persons, who jointly assume the responsibility of bringing into the world other human persons, should be ready to insure for these new beings the elementary minimum of security, care, education, etc., particularly in the face of their frailty and impotence during the long period of their slow development into adults. Here again modern psychology endorses a dictate of common sense. Generally speaking, the emotional balance and the character of the child do not depend merely on a superficial stability or mere economic status of the parental couple, but also and more directly on the true worth of their love for one another. And that child is most likely to be well-balanced whose parents love each other so perfectly that the indissolubility and oneness of their union is utterly beyond question. To state the matter conversely, parents who love each other well enough to give their child an ideal emotional balance can have for each other nothing but a permanent and exclusive love. Of itself and to be itself, love demands to be untrammelled by any concern as to how long it will last, and whether it will ebb or come to an end. Curiously enough, the infant, even before the age of reason, responds to this fact quite sharply in its emotional impressionability, however dim and unconscious it may be.

Here, it seems, is a consideration on which it is worth while for us to dwell. In his first years the child's life is basically made up of impulses and reactions of an emotional nature. The harmonious evolution of these processes will lay the proper psychological foundation for the building and balanced development of the child's ultimate intellectual and spiritual personality. Hence, the immense practical importance of these first years and of the emotional climate which surrounds their unfolding. This climate is a dependent variable, in most cases, of the relations which control the persons in the child's immediate environment; above all, its parents. The most apparent feature of this entire first period of the child's life up to 8 years is in the main an absolute need to be loved and to feel secure. Feelings of either frustration or satisfaction of this need are experienced without shadings of any degree, directly and absolutely; they have at times such deep repercussions that the individual will never be able in later life to rid himself entirely, for instance, of certain anguish complexes incurred at this initial stage of his emotional life. Any dissension between the parents is generally felt by the child as a threat to its emotional security, and as a frustration of its need for untroubled love. Moreover, the mutual love of the parents one for the other is of the essence if the child is to be able to renounce exclusive attachment to one or the other parent and quietly to identify itself with the parent of its own sex. To be harmful, disagreements between parents need not be of an explosive nature or a spectacular display; dearth of love persisting in dreary silence between parents who live "side by side" without real intimacy is enough to create for the child an emotional climate comparable to a permanent void, which it is obviously unable either to analyze or to escape. Such dissension is the source of real drama or conflict. As an example of this it is enough to cite what takes place during the so-called Oedipus complex period. At that time the child is more attracted to the parent of the opposite sex, and in a sense prefers this parent. If the child perceives the parent of its own sex as inflicting pain on the favorite parent, the child's reaction will be ambivalent: love, arising from a sense of dependency, for the parent of the opposite sex and hatred for the other parent of its own sex. As a consequence the child starts out in life with an emotional bias which may well forever plague all normal relations with persons of the subject's own sex, and also with persons of the opposite sex because, for example, of some unavowed sense of inferiority.

Daily clinical experience reveals clearly what a profoundly unfavorable impact such imbalance in parental understanding can have on the psychology of the child. The father's contempt for the mother may create in the offspring a disposition to despise womanhood; fickleness or brutality in the father may arouse in the child homosexual tendencies, conscious or not, which will more or less grievously encumber the child's psychic make-up in eventual adulthood; or again, a child who is witness to a father's simultaneous violence and sensuousness toward the mother may develop a sadistic complex which may possibly never be shed entirely. Who can tell the number of these secret conflicts of which only the priest-confessor or the professional specialist becomes aware? Statistics reveal a startling fact on this point: the incidence of trouble in character adjustment is more than five times greater in children of disorganized families, particularly where divorce has occurred, than in children of normal households.

The emotional and psychological development of a child is a long and difficult matter. Relations between children themselves eventually come to complicate the process or to help it along according to circumstances, especially according to the degree of union of the parents. Education is a delicate task, demanding continual attention not so much to different educational theories as to the all-important fact that if the parents are really concerned with their children's proper growth from every point of view, they must begin by truly loving one another with complete reciprocity, with mindful respect, and with a genuine charity. Further, they must love their children as human persons and not as mere things or as charming little dolls that happen to be alive. All this requires in each parent the sacrifice of the die-hard egoistic impulse to recover one's "liberty," or to seek outside the conjugal union emotional compensations of a questionable nature.

The love which unites the parents is the force that brings about procreation from the biological point of view; but it must go further, and fashion from the child the adult human being who will himself be able in due time, with full consciousness of his action and with complete mastery over his emotional reflexes, to bring forth in turn other new living beings. The child is the flowering, in the fullest and most complete sense of that word, of parental union in marital love. The procreative function in its real significance requires this love first to procreate, and then to complete fully the work for which it was ordained. Without love the procreative act amounts not to an animal function, as is often said, but really to something sub-animal; its disorder being so complete that it no longer has any relation to the vital order of nature. Such is the awesome price of liberty pawned, the utter perversion of a created mind defaulting in the mission assigned to it by the Creator. The most frightening aspect of this whole disorder is the fact that its consequences are often not at once evident to those who waywardly bring it on. In the face of the astounding confusion about the meaning of the word love—a word bestowed thoughtlessly on either amatory dalliance, the joys of true fraternity, prostitution, conjugal spirituality, mystical life or even the very life of God—how many Christians have understood with complete lucidity that sexuality cannot be accepted unless it meets all the standards of love in the sense of the Gospel context? Or how many Christians are really aware of the fact that love alone is the really ultimate obligation, that sex is but a particular modality of love, the procreative modality in the fullest meaning of the word, and that if from certain external reasons there should arise a conflict between love and the sexual need it is the latter that must yield?

The fundamental demands of love

There exists no such thing as an individual being totally isolated within itself. Such a being can be no more than an abstract subject of rationalization, and even then it can be defined only in relation to other beings or other categories of beings. Only the manner in which a thing differs from others about it allows us to recognize it precisely as a distinct individual.

With even greater reason there exist, in the realm of living beings, only singular and particular beings which are established in their existence by their relations to other beings. I exist only because there lies about me a universe which sustains me, feeds me, causes me to think; and this universe seen as a whole is but a concatenation, an extremely complex system of mutual relationships, itself kept in existence only by its essential relation to God the Creator.

In the animal world, though the individual possesses a certain self-determination in this relational universe and a degree of autonomy because he is endowed with sense perception, the exercise of the vital relations is regulated by the automation of instinct. In the world of man, however, these relations are motivated solely by love and free will, instinct being reduced here to a mere prompting impulse. Each human person is individually capable of setting in motion his forces of relation, or of refusing to move them, or of causing them to deviate. He may direct them toward another fellow being and assign to them this other person as their goal; and this is the normal procedure in forming a community. But man is also capable of bending these forces back toward himself in a kind of obsessive pursuit which in a way attempts to give the lie to the real structure of the universe. Here, in this strange capacity of man to retire within himself and shut himself off from reality, we encounter one of the great mysteries of the human enigma. For it seems that love, the powerful force out of which the whole human community is to be fashioned, somehow or other contains an inscrutable inertia whose origins reason cannot uncover. And though its existence must be accepted for the sake of objectivity, it still remains inexplicable.

Man's selfishness is really a mystery. A mystery, indeed, but a universal fact encountered in every sphere of human life. People are always set slightly at loggerheads by the injection of self into their mutual relations. We are inclined to project upon someone else, without awareness and often in genuinely good faith, a fanciful image of ourselves —one which is either wishful thinking and nostalgic yearning or rejection of some disturbing tendencies of our own. By the same token, the other person finds himself somewhat diminished and cut down in his true reality, however, legitimately he desires to be recognized for what he is. Hence there arise misunderstandings and conflicts which are the sharper in proportion as the projection is unconscious on our part and misleads even ourselves. Is there anyone who is not vexed at not finding in his fellow-worker, his friend or even his enemy certain traits of character or behavior patterns he fancied as rightfully to be expected? Is there anyone who is not annoyed by the discovery that the woman he loves is *herself*, in the sense that her real personality, whose richness he had inadvertently failed to notice, does not necessarily correspond to his ideal preconceived concept of it: an ideal born, whether he admits it or not, of his own egocentric needs? If we could but enjoy total liberty of mind to permit us to see our neighbor in the fullness of his proper personality, without the slightest projection of ourselves, we could then love him as totally distinct from ourselves, in a network of fully developed personal relations, and there would not be any problems of morality, of sociology, or of psychology. This clinging, as it were, of ourselves to our own selfish desires is possibly the most tangible and basic result of original sin.

Now if man wants to play his part in this relational world, give it every benefit of his capacity of self-donation while at the same time he finds in it his best chances of genuine personal growth—in this world of time as well as in the gratuitously offered world of eternity—he must spend his days rooting out of himself, painfully if need be, the narcissistic indolence which is in him. So strong and seductive is this inertia arising from inordinate love of self that for man to stir out of it he must make a powerful act of faith in the eventual possibility of the development of his human resources, a development which he can only faintly foresee. Thus for a twenty-year-old to be able to separate the woman he loves from his own ideal image of her, for him to set out deliberately with her on a two-person quest for a kind of joy about which he himself has not too clear a notion, and for him to renounce immediate joys in favor of jointly reaching for another unknown joy said to be greater—such a man must have attained an extremely high and rare degree of personal freedom.

It remains true that the sexual function, above all others, deeply involves the relational character of life, and therefore that sex will most urgently demand detachment from narcissism under pain of failure on man's part to keep in step with humanity's march forward. It is, however, in sexual matters that narcissism is at its strongest, its most subtle and its most unavowed degree of activity. Therefore in this sphere of sex, a privileged experience of love, man's readiness to adjust to the relational structure of the world will be the result of his most strenuous effort to be free of self-love. Sexuality essentially involves love, therefore it involves self-imposed regulation, and therefore it calls for a moral code.

Short of renouncing his mission as man, and of consenting to the disintegration of his moral life, man must love. This means that man, while he reserves to himself a degree of self-determination in his estimate of values, must choose to conform his behavior to the sovereign laws of nature and to the calls of grace. He shall not separate sex from procreation, either in principle or in his judgment of the principle; he shall not set for himself a concept of procreation as independent of love, or call upon laboratory techniques to substitute for life. Of course he *can*, he *is able*, to do such things—just as he can kill or mutilate himself; he can, as did André Gide, put falsehood in the place of truth; he can entertain illusions which would blot out and eclipse the great radiance of his responsibility. But in so doing he is objectively and factually in rebellion against the order of the world, which is tantamount to being in revolt against the will of God Himself.*

Again, use of the sexual function solely and exclusively to express and prove mutual affection would be counter to the supernatural character of this function as made resplendent by the sacrament of marriage. Such an exercise of the sex function would also be a capitulation to illusory self-love, to a kind of double or reciprocal narcissism, deceitfully hidden under the name of love.

The sacred character of sexuality

In the Christian view, the fact of sex assumes new greatness and importance, and this leads one to understand why the Church has never consented to look upon sex as a secondary, unimportant factor in the sphere of morality. The traditional moral teaching of the Church holds that any offense in mat-

---

* This does not mean he will always be in rebellion subjectively and in his own mind, with explicit awareness of repeated choices between fulfilling his mission or defaulting in it. We are speaking here only of principle. Later we shall look more closely at man in the concrete, man divided against himself, drawn here and there, hesitant and often made to suffer anguish in his struggle in time.

ters of sex is in principle a serious infringement of essentials; though in the case of individual concrete lapses this may not always and necessarily be so, by reason of possible extenuation of personal responsibility.

The sexual function in man is the power to carry the love and union between two persons to the point of creating new life. Sexual instinct is therefore a distinct impulse to creative love.

What we are now about to say should in no way shock the reader, or give him any reason to involve himself in any sort of eccentric spirituality. To avoid both these pitfalls let us, as we develop our reflections, keep firmly in mind as guidemarks two absolute truths: first, that God is the Infinite, non-corporeal Being; and second, that sexuality as a biological function rather than a source of psychological differentiation between individuals has to do with our temporal existence on earth. With these two points kept clearly in mind, we should readily agree that there is a singular and striking analogy between God, as He reveals Himself to us in the intimate mystery of His relations, and the meaning of sexuality. To be quite exact let us add that the analogy is an altogether general and rather distant one.

Theology tells us that the mystery of the Trinity is the affirmation of personal relations in God, Who might be spoken of as "three infinite and absolutely distinct Persons loving one another infinitely so that they are but one Being, 'Love'" or, again, as the supreme and infinitely perfect mode of relational life. Now, as we have seen, the unfolding of life in man, is also of a relational order though in a very imperfect and limited way. It amounts, therefore, only to a commonplace to say that in all domains what makes creation possible is the union of different persons, whereas absolute and willful solitude is ultimately sterile; and in its narcissistic form (as practiced by Gide) even self-destructive.

Of all the natural realms where relational life unfolds sexuality is the one which gains its grandeur by its analogy to the life of God, for here the fusing of two persons results, on the very strength of the function itself, in the creation of a community which is itself creative. It is often said that the child is the living proof and materialization or, so to speak, the extension of the love of its parents. True as this may be in a sense, it is truer still to realize that above all the child is *itself*, a new living mystery, a personal being who has a personal destiny to achieve, who is the subject of relations with others who must command respect, and who broadens to truly social dimensions the community originally constituted by the parents, who themselves are always prone to be more or less wrapped up in themselves and each other. The child is charged with a particular and singular potentiality, and faces a future which no one else may rightfully appropriate —an important fact which parents tend too often to forget and for too-long periods. Having reached adulthood, this third person will start the cycle anew, extending it to others who are not "of the family," when his time comes in turn for the choosing of a mate who also will come bearing the burden and the potentialities of a radically different background. The very fact that sexuality is the biological function of procreation clearly shows that it exists for a reality broader than mere self, namely, for the human community. It also shows that if anyone should attempt to make of sex a goal in itself, despoiling it of its subordination to the extension of the species, he would be contradicting the inmost nature of sexuality itself.

It was stated previously that the sex instinct is an impulse to creative love. Now the absolute in creative love is the Triune God; and as an intrinsically social function the sexual mode of relational life is precisely analogous at its specific level and in temporal life to God's own inner life. Every living being participates each in its own limited measure in God's power to create through love; and man does so at his spiritual level according to the measure of his free will. Such a sharing of power is not the least of God's gifts! And it is in this perspective that a Christian, conscious of his faith, ought to see his sexual instinct and power, guide their exercise, and give them the highest possible degree of conformity with God's way.

This is not an attempt to divinize sexuality. We were careful in earlier discussion to warn the reader of the danger of false spirituality, precisely because some writers, anxious to rehabilitate marriage where its spiritual and sacramental aspects are too often unappreciated or disregarded, have at times been ambiguous in this matter. A balanced conjugal spirituality requires for its foundation a very accurate perception of this analogy to the Trinity. In seeking to spiritualize his sexuality man must understand it in its proper significance, that of a temporal sharing for the sake of human society in the generative Love which is God. What is further needed for man is the exact sense of his own limits and of those which circumscribe his sexuality.

Theologians of the Eastern and the Western Churches are still in opposition regarding the question of how the Holy Ghost proceeds from the Father and the Son. We state in our Western creed, without further particulars, that He does proceed from the Father and the Son. But the creed of the Eastern rites specifies that He proceeds from the Father and the Word *as from one principle*; in other words, it is the union of the first two persons of the Trinity which causes the third to spring forth. Incidentally, these two theological views were officially reconciled twice in history, first at the Council of Lyons in 1274, and again at the Council of Florence in 1439.

Though they are points of theological argument, these views are important in helping us to grasp more clearly the fact that the divine life in which we are called to share in Christ is not a simple juxtaposition but rather an absolute and dynamic unity.

On this precise point modern psychology suggests to us another aspect of the remote but real analogy of conjugal love to the love in God. The simple juxtaposition of two self-seeking human beings of complementary sex can always, biologically, result in the birth of a child; but for this offspring to develop maximum soundness in its emotional structure the parents must be more than mere egoists, singly or jointly. They must be truly united in love, in reciprocal giving, in perfect relationship characterized by maximum avoidance of self-indulgence in the realm of instinct. Such a love must on occasion

V

even know enough to transcend and sublimate the sexual instinct.

"Be perfect, even as your heavenly Father is perfect." Imitator of God, seeking to conform with Him Who is subsistent Love, the married Christian can do no better than orient and guide, according to this precept, the awe-inspiring power he has for loving, even to the point of creating a human person.

3

On the Purposes
of Marriage

IN ORDER to take a fresh approach to
the matter of the various ends for which marriage
exists, we might sum up all our preceding observa-
tions by saying that the voluntary and free character
of man's activity implies, if man is to consent to the
established order of things, the need for man to give
definite direction to the various instinctive, emotional, and voluntary forces of his being. Thus the
human being is free to direct his sexual life toward
some goal of which he must be at least implicitly
aware. And no act, including the sex act, if given
over to the mere chance of nervous or organic impulses would be really human; nor could any part
of sexual activity which might elude the control or
the direction of free will be qualified, in the full
sense of the word, as human.

The goal toward which man must direct his acts
is not subject to his choice but rests in an established
order of things. Man must come to know this goal
and heed the established order, or else he will not
be in tune with the laws of his nature. Now sexual-

ity in man is the source of an emotional movement of the psychological order which students of the subject call "the tender emotion," as well as of a pleasurable excitation of the nervous system termed "erotic pleasure," both phenomena manifesting themselves on the occasion of the exercise of a biological function whose end is procreation. The first has direct relation to what is highest in man's spiritual nature; one might even say it is the most intense actual experiencing of his spirituality in the natural register, provided it implies genuine tenderness and not merely selfish passion. As for the second phenomenon it is, morally speaking, neutral or indifferent; that is to say it becomes good or evil only in relation to the first; and it becomes an evil and a hindrance for man as soon as it ceases to be ordained to his higher spiritual nature. Indeed, the tyranny of sheer carnal indulgence comes close to being as oppressive a tyranny as drug addiction.

Various concepts of the goals of marriage

Taking into account various existing philosophical and religious preconceptions, one can distinguish more than a few approaches to the study of the aims of marriage. Such schemes are obviously not all of equal worth.

An authentically human biology, and by that we mean a biology that refuses to consider man a mere animal, cannot accept the setting of the goal of marriage in simple hedonistic terms. To look upon marriage as merely the official and socially sanctioned way to sexual enjoyment of the marital partner is to disregard not only the biological reality of sex but also the psychological aspects of the emotional instinct associated with sex. Such a view of marriage is much more prevalent than one thinks, if not in these simplistic terms, at least at the partial component of a more complex attitude. It enters all too often, unfortunately, into the presentation to young people of an ostensibly "Christian morality" when it takes the form of this admonition: "Until you are married, be careful when you are with girls (or, with boys); restrain yourself until marriage; after that . . . you will be entirely free!" The implication that marriage is a state in which, granting one observes some basic decencies, sex is at last going to be indulged, is not too rare a notion even among well-meaning Christians. There could not, of course, be a more unsound and misleading mental and emotional preparation for marriage than this, especially when it is graced with tones of morality.

Also to be dismissed as an expression of the goal of marriage is the notion that marriage is a state of life one adopts for reasons of "social conformity." This view is much less fashionable today than it was formerly, but there are still some men who, having lived a life of independence and having never really committed themselves in their youth, now toy with the idea of "ending it all," by marrying a not-too-unattractive woman who seems able to assure healthy progeny (the family name must be carried on!) and to whom they can be unfaithful without too much fuss whenever they once again have the urge "to play the field." Such an envisagement of the facts and goals of marriage is perhaps even more revolting than the first because it is so cold, rational-

istic, and selfish. On the other hand, a woman sometimes enters marriage under the influence of emotional disturbance, whether conscious or not. This
situation occurs more frequently than is commonly
suspected. The woman, in short, wants a child to
love dearly and, it may be added, quite possessively.
Such a desire would not of itself involve any great
aberration, except for the fact that in this emotional
complex, arising from certain conflicts of which she
is unaware, a woman does not fully accept the sexual condition of being a woman, but rather looks
upon it as she would a condition of inferiority. And
to her, the child she can have represents a compensation: either a proof that she is not really inferior, or a means of bringing into play her repressed emotions. The child appears to her to be
the object of her deepest desires. This abnormal
craving may even go so far as to lead her to resort
to artificial insemination or to consider the adoption
of a child. It may more simply dispose her to want
marriage as the means of having a child; and in
this situation the man is regarded by her only as the
one legal instrumentality by which she can be sure
to have a child *of her own.* According to the degree
of education or religious conviction of such a
woman, the deep underlying intention will be more
or less conscious, avowed, or hidden behind the
edifying screen of the maternal instinct. In cases of
this kind it is quite obvious that the aims of sexual
union or marriage are viewed only as the gratifying
of an abnormal and excessively self-centered instinct of possession and not as the expression of
love aiming at procreation.

When the discussion of the aims of marriage

stems from considerations on the plane of nature pure and simple, and full account is taken of all the elements, both biological and psychological, involved in an understanding of man, it may be said that marriage is ordained to the establishment of a mutual association based on love. Thus marriage is committed to procreation under such conditions as shall be most advantageous to the child. In this state man and woman find full flowering and mutual joy, through a truly creative love.

This last statement of the aims of marriage, however, becomes inadequate the moment we enlarge this purely natural scope to the infinite proportions that God's revealed word has established. Now, and on this new supernatural plane, marriage must be oriented to the transcendent reality of the Mystical Body, the Church Triumphant, and marriage becomes a sacrament. The single and sovereign purpose of every human activity is to prepare and build in time this transcendent reality. And this is why the sacraments are made available, and each is intended to direct a particular phase of man's activity. Such are the ends of the Sacrament of marriage with regard to the human sex instinct.

At this point we are faced with an apparent contradiction in the assertions of moral theologians, and even in the official teachings of the Church. In the discussion of the goals of marriage two purposes are ranged side by side, and though both have respective merit, they seem at first glance to be opposed: paradoxically indeed, if one of these aims is insisted upon to the exclusion of the other, discussion can very easily reach a deadlock. The first view is that procreation is the primary end of marriage; whereas the second insists upon assigning that role to mutual love between the mates.

It must be said in passing that the terms in this theological controversy are very much lacking in precision and are often even ambiguous. When, for example, it is said that the "primary" end of the "union" of man and woman is procreation, what is the meaning of the word *primary* in this statement, and in what perspective should the word *union* be considered?

This dialectical trend can be detected even in the encyclical "*Casti connubii,*" for this document affirms the priority of the procreative end of marriage while teaching at the same time that the first reason for marriage is the mutual perfecting of the spouses with love, of course, as the substratum. St. Augustine declares that "woman should not marry, except to become a mother," but in another connection he asserts that the real value of Christian marriage lies in the fact that it is like a seminary or school which prepares man for entrance into the City of God; and that in this respect it surpasses the good of procreation. To validate this latter view he points out that the exclusiveness of the marriage bond cannot be violated for the purpose of having a child. And for St. Thomas, the intimate love and union of two persons are evidently the essential requisites to the begetting of new immortal persons under conditions most favorable to their development.

Even this brief reference to the position of the two greatest doctors of the Church is sufficient to make us see clearly that both goals of marriage are stressed. And the Church itself, in the various documents of its teaching, emphasizes as much as is

necessary the Christian demand that neither of the
two aims be set aside, and that one should not be
minimized in order to give priority to the other.
Nevertheless, all these various teachings are in general embodied in terms which are quite technical,
more or less philosophical in character, and sometimes even foreign to the ways of the modern mind.
The Abbé Lochet, however, in a remarkable article
in the *Nouvelle Revue Théologique*, May and June
1951, has provided an interesting synthesis, in modern terms, of this twofold approach to the question
of the purposes of marriage, and has made what
clearly is an important contribution to reflection on
the matter.

From his article it becomes clear that marriage
is, in the highest degree, that specifically human
reality called a society, a union of free persons motivated to work in common. Now every society moves
toward two goals of very different nature. The first
is the social goal, that of simply acting as a group
in a collaboration the value of which is dependent
upon the variable quality of the pooled resources;
the second is the goal of communality whereby each
member thrives and is perfected in union with other
persons. To take an example, we may cite an alumni
association which by agreement meets once a month
for a dinner. The social goal is the meal itself; but
the goal of communality is the meeting and uniting
with schoolmates in order to share memories, friendships, and the new attainments each one may have
realized through his profession and experience.

In marriage, the social end depends upon the
good which is specific to this association, namely,
the mutual sharing of sexuality, and will therefore

be the procreation of children. The purpose of communality will be the conscious sharing and exchanging of anything else it is possible for the mates to give to each other. Thus husband and wife will prepare themselves for that perfect community, which is transcendent and eternal, the Mystical Body, through the translation of Love into human terms, a translation which God's grace has raised to the level of a sacrament. Here is a true example of the way in which God gives infinite proportions to a natural capacity as He makes human procreative power the very condition for the building and increase of the Mystical Body.

One cannot, therefore, compare these two goals as to their respective value or importance, since the first has regard to time and the second to eternity. One purpose does not interfere with the other—far from it; for it is in attaining the perfection of the first and temporal aim that attainment of the second, the eternal one, is assured. This is all the more true, since we know from Christ's own words that sexuality as a function will not exist when time ceases to be. We should, therefore, never limit the goal of the sexual union to simple and quasi-animal and biological reproduction; nor, on the other hand, should we take as eternal something which is only temporal, and imagine that the sensual as well as the emotional joy of the specifically sexual union of the partners, however great its moral good or its worth as proof and manifestation of love, can, as such, have eternal values. Of itself, the sexual function is directed to a very precise social end, unless one is disposed to deny the elementary facts of nature. Nevertheless, in a certain sense it enters closely into the frame of a society which transcends it, but which still receives from it its specific character as a society. There is consequently need for a very sharp distinction between the two ends and their relationship to each other, for without this distinction grave confusions will result.

To state this in other terms and in conformity with all the biological, psychological and spiritual data of the problem, one might say that two persons of different sex, mutually attracted to each other by the mysterious force of their instinct or their love, will freely constitute an association of official and definitive character—hence legal, contractual aspect of marriage—and will place in common the reciprocal offering of their generative sexual power. In the very complex daily workings of this association and of their love, which involves many other things besides strictly sexual acts, they are to prepare themselves for their eventual destiny in heaven. Through their concrete and specific use of sexual union they come to make it into a creative collaboration, for even though the aim of marriage in general is love in the fullest meaning of the word, it nevertheless remains true that sexuality in marriage, as the particular expression of this love, keeps procreation as its end. A Christian and well-balanced view cannot allow itself to be blinded to the fact that sexuality itself is not the ultimate factor.

In a third modification of our statement we might say that marriage is clearly a particular and privileged form of preparation during life on earth for perfect charity; and that, just as clearly, marriage is specifically directed to procreation. * It would be just as inaccurate to say that a person marries only for love, as to state that one marries only to have children. Distinction can therefore be made between the proximate goal, which is procreation, and the ultimate end, which is the exercise of mutual love. This brings us back to traditional terminology, and we can therefore declare that the primary end of marriage is procreation—sexuality being immediately a procreative function—and that the mutual love of the partners is secondary as an end only in terms of logic but not, of course, in spiritual importance.

In occasional instances and by mere accident nature itself may rule out the procreative end, independently of the will of the married couple. The situation is then one of inadequacy, one simply to be accepted, as when, for example, a woman becomes sterile through sickness or age. The normal couple cannot deliberately go against the laws of nature in making sexuality serve to release a nervous and emotional tension in a sexual act wherein it would deliberately set aside the possible achievement of the procreative goal. For true love, as it really must be understood in the vital order of the universe, could never be called upon to justify such a definite negating of that order itself. This is why the Church so uncompromisingly insists on the inherently immoral character of all contraceptive practices.

---

* See, for instance, the decree of the Holy Office of April 1, 1944, on the ends of marriage, *Acta Sanctae Sedis*, Vol. 36, p. 103. Against the thesis of Doms, the Church insists on the primacy of the procreative end of marriage.

And conception of a child outside the dynamism of true sexual love is viewed by the Church as a gross distortion of human nature. For this reason the Church has condemned artificial insemination, inasmuch as it is intended to replace the normal sexual union of a couple.

Further, the intention to use sex only for one's personal sensual pleasure is looked upon by the Church as something equally monstrous. St. Thomas even goes so far as to say that contraceptive practices are, strictly speaking, just as much against the natural order—in a moral, but not a psychological, sense of course—as homosexuality. All such acts are transgressions in that they constitute behavior which is out of harmony with the reality of the normal order that presides over sexuality in general. Whether these acts are always and automatically mortal sins is another question entirely, and one we shall examine later. However, they are certainly lapses from temperance—the virtue concerned with the rule of the life of the senses; and in this particular aspect lapses from chastity—the virtue specifically concerned with genital sensuality. But they are also failures in regard to love itself, for in spite of whatever illusions of tenderness and generosity the couple might entertain, such conduct inevitably downgrades each one in his quality as a person when one reduces the other to the level of a mere instrument of selfish pleasure by a deliberate abridgment of their joint generative power. In this sublime domain, as soon as precedence is given to sensual enjoyment over all else, the very biological and psychological make-up of a human being inevitably brings about a resurgence in him of egocentricity not only in the play of his instincts but even further and eventually in his overall behavior. Couples who live in habitual practice of contraception cannot but suffer impairment in their vital balance as a couple. Though some of these marriages might at first appear to be successful, they can be easily seen to be built on temporary working-compromises between two egotistical parties devoid of real love. In this regard we are, of course, referring solely to couples who are unconcerned about marital values, and we have no intention of condemning couples who are in a tragic struggle with difficulties they cannot always surmount. It would, however, be an error to think that the single solution offered by the practice of contraception will ease the tensions which inevitably arise when a couple is faced with the necessity of delaying the birth of a child. The same is true of the systematic practice of *amplexus reservatus.* * The practice by mutual agreement of what is commonly known as "the rhythm" does not, however, present this danger, since the entire unfolding of sexual reflexes remains in this instance entirely normal. Provided such periodic continence according to the law of Ogino is not intended to eliminate forever the possibility of having children, and does not turn into the quest of sexual pleasure for its own sake—even under cover of this or that "emotional" and "spiritual" rationalization—then this practice of Oginism has of itself no particular moral overtones, since it is intrinsically neither good nor evil.

---

* See footnote, p. 20.

The suggestions found in the Scriptures

It should be of interest to dwell for a moment on the first biblical texts on this question of the goals of marriage.

The first story of Creation, having set forth the beauty and wealth of God's creative gift, places particular emphasis on the fact that the resemblance of the human being to God comprises a differentiation into two persons dedicated to a mutual union so as to be fruitful together. It does not appear to be an unwarranted interpretation of the sacred text to say that the distinction between sexes with the creative result of their coming together offers a real though imperfect analogy to divine life itself, an analogy further to be clarified by the later revelation of the mystery of the Trinity. Moreover, God's first command bears on man's duty to be fruitful (Genesis 1:28).

The second story proceeds inversely. It is man, the male, who first appears in the world; he is alone and in a way undifferentiated. The whole universe has been created for him, yet it immediately appears that there must be a splitting of man into two parts, and that the human being must be of two distinct persons pledged to seek union with each other. The achieving of resemblance with God required in some way that this spiritual being be made of two distinct individuals in quest of community existence.

It seems therefore that Scripture itself stresses the two goals of the union of man and woman. Yet one cannot ascribe to the magnificent words of Genesis

2:24 an exclusively sexual significance. In the text "they shall be two in one flesh," the word "flesh" should not be taken in the sense it has in the expression "sins of the flesh"; it must be assumed to have the meaning in which St. Paul takes it, excluding at once a properly supernatural reference, but also the pride which, after the fall, resists God's spirit at work within us. The oneness in the flesh which Genesis shows us as the goal by the Creator Himself is infinitely more extensive than the mere carrying out of the reproductive function; it is the fulfillment of the primary potentiality of the couple acting in its totally combined capacity. Nothing in the biblical narrative can justify the assumption that the procreative sexual function as such should be the most important element in marital unity.

There follows in the Scriptures the whole unfolding of Mosaic legislation, which is very clear-cut as to sexual relationships. It must not be taken from Moses' precepts that sexuality as such is condemned as evil, or that the pleasure and joy in sexual union are regarded as being tainted to their roots with wickedness. All the commands of the Mosaic law pivot on the view that in the fall from grace attendant upon original sin man's attraction to sexual enjoyment has become inordinate to the point that this enticement shows a strong tendency—as do all allurements of the senses—to make man bog down in the quicksands of an exclusively temporal outlook. They stunt his spiritual growth, thereby turning him away from his true destiny. Thus man, having heard the call of Jahweh, will have to set out on a course of progress and activity of every kind in order to escape the arrested development which sensual pleasure for its own sake always threatens to bring about. He must learn to free himself from the slavery of sexual intoxication, which is particularly heady; but he must also learn to use the intoxication itself, because as created by God it is good and ought to be used in its proper place and as a symbol, however imperfect, of a higher reality, the total union of persons. It took the entire and progressive education of the chosen people at the hands of God throughout the Old Testament to reach true spirituality in marriage: a spirituality described in all its luminous clarity by Christ Himself and by St. Paul. Christ actually said that in ancient times men were not ready for a complete understanding of this spirituality when he explained to the Pharisees why Moses had permitted them to write a notice of dismissal and put away their wives (Mark 10:2–9; Matthew 19:7–9).

This long education culminated in the clear Gospel affirmation of the temporal character of sexuality as a function, for Christ declared to the Sadducees that "at the resurrection they will neither marry nor be given in marriage" (Matthew 22:29–30).

And St. Paul goes so far as to declare that the prototype of the unity of marital love is the union of our Lord and His Church, an old biblical theme which goes as far back at least as the *Canticle of Canticles*. Moreover, he points out that true Christians who have finally understood by the grace of the Word Incarnate the true meaning of their vocation in Christ Jesus cannot allow themselves to be seized by the giddiness of temporal and sensory things, especially by sexual intoxication desired for its own sake. To do so would constitute an attitude of deliberate lust, in one of the forms St. Paul enumerates as examples of immoral conduct in the *First Epistle to the Corinthians*.

Scripture therefore presents an immense synthesis of all the aspects of man's dynamic activity, and particularly of its most intense aspect, sexuality. In the course of centuries, the Church will do no more than restate this synthesis in explicit terms, according to the special needs of the day. Christian conjugal morality is by no means merely a series of prohibitions; on the contrary, its directives are affirmative, precise, and exhaustive in the highest conceivable degree.

4

The Ideal Marital Union

HAVING CONSIDERED the concrete conditions proper to man himself, to his organism, his social adjustment and his own proper ends, we are now in a position to evolve a more exact concept of what the ideal union between man and woman should be.

Primordially "divided," as it were, into two distinct persons destined to beget a third person through their own union with each other, the human being spends his earthly and temporal life seeking an unachieved and often even jeopardized unity, a stability as yet unattained, a fulfillment he feels is peculiarly fated to be his. In a natural and well-ordered view of things, the dynamic unity for this quest shall depend on the married couple as such.

The need for acting as adults

The ideal couple receives its definition in the complete, definitive, and free (*i.e.*, responsible and spontaneous) exchange of gifts between two adult and well-developed persons of complementary sexes.

A truism? Of course, but some of these notions always require our reexamination.

Sex is not just a certain physical, anatomical and functional conformation. It is a condition involving and influencing the entire person in the emotions, in the ways of thinking and judging, in the whole frame of reference within which the person chooses to view the world and life. Sex represents a person's psychological approach to the implementing of relationships and of all activity. A man is not really a man, capable therefore of really and effectively loving a woman, unless he has fully and consciously acquired certain powers of initiative, conquest, strength of leadership, without faltering before the demands such powers make upon him, but also without straining them to the point where they become a sort of "will to power" tantamount to the reassertion of an inferiority complex. On the other hand, a woman is not fully capable of playing the part of a woman unless she has fully understood and accepted womanhood with its features of active receptivity, of need for support coupled with the special gift of intuitive perception so indispensable to the equilibrium of the mated pair; above all, she must understand and accept motherhood: her exalted part in the glorious task of procreation, a part burdened with the most exacting demands.

It is therefore necessary for both persons, man and woman, to enjoy maximum release from the confused unconscious yearnings of frustrated childhood emotionalism. Such release will forestall a constant, if unwitting, tendency to seek in their married life compensations for this or that deficiency which might have plagued their early emotional life within their respective families. In other words, each partner must consider the other as a person really *other* and distinct, one to whom the gift of oneself is complete and mutual, not as an ill-defined part of a person who might fill the void created by the frustration of some childhood emotional need. The power of each to love should be at the peak of spontaneity, immune to any instinctive self-regard—an attitude which is all the more deceiving since it always takes on the more or less vivid appearance of what is called "love," though it is nothing more than an unreasonable, self-centered demand.

The need for being realistic

It is also essential to the proper balance of a married couple that neither mate should fall victim to idealism or to illusions about the other. This means that the bright joy of their mutual "find" should not so dazzle them as to leave them blind to the irreducible element of frailty in every human being on this earthly pilgrimage. There persists in each of us so great a thirst for success, so deep a desire for the absolute that we remain quite impervious to the reality of failure or of conflict in daily life. If we possess but for a fleeting moment the joy of love in all its purity and grandeur, we irresistibly tend to settle down in it and to believe it is with us to stay, by virtue of its own power, acquired, solid and lasting. This is perhaps the most cruel and stubborn illusion to which we fall prey. In point of fact, our joys exist only so long as we keep creating them, and they crumble away the moment we fail to keep activating them with creative energy, with a constant effort to extend ourselves, to move forward, foregoing the moment just past, thrilling though it was, in order to prepare for the next moment which is always more fraught with demands and weighted down with difficulties.

No doubt the most subtle danger is that of a certain idealism which tends to assign to sexual union, for its own sake, first rank in the scale of values, especially spiritual values, in marriage. Again, in actual fact there is no couple, granted its parties are sincere persons, that has not been aware as much of the immeasurable significance of sex as of its terrible inadequacy. This is because sexuality alone is not everything; but it is also a consequence of the strong tendency, deeply rooted in each one of the spouses, to be sluggishly self-centered and powerless to wrench oneself free from narcissism or self-love. Each partner in varying degree is forever busy looking for self in the other, most of the time unwittingly and in good faith; but if two people should hurry into married life with blissful disregard of the fact that they have this weakness, they would be heading into a spiritual impasse, or riding for a tragic fall. Not only their spiritual relationship but their sexual instinct itself, as we shall see, would be saddled with this burden of selfishness; and their very reflexes would be at odds, now impelling them to altruistic love and to gift of self to one another, now holding them back with invincibly selfish reactions. In order to prevent all this, a call must be made at the very outset of married life upon the quiet and objective kind of courage it takes to admit the basic fact that man is selfish, a fact which is quite unpalatable to anyone's self-esteem. Psychologists might describe this weakness as a result of arrested development in instinctive emotional life, or as an inability to attain at all levels of human activity, whether spontaneous or half-conscious or deliberate, the freedom to give oneself and to separate oneself from one's own egotistic desires. It is this freedom which constitutes the supreme balance in human personality.

That specific frailty of man is the basis for the struggle St. Paul describes in his *Epistle to the Romans* (7:15–20). A disregard of the practical importance of this real weakness, which is partly moral decay and partly a regressive yearning, would be the surest preparation for soul-searing setbacks, as much in the moral as in the emotional complexes of a married couple.

The need for being constructive

Union in marriage can be thought of only as a matter of long and arduous construction on the part of two people and as a result of their joint efforts. Such an observation may seem to be a commonplace; but the point demands emphasis.

It seems, indeed, that in current evaluations of marriage—not so much ones expressly stated as those underlying the habitual behavior of people—marriage is quite often considered as "a settling down," or as a terminus. How very many young people there are who have in their student days, for example, led a life morally and spiritually well-directed toward the vaguely foreseen eventuality of marriage, with an unhampered disposition some day to give themselves to another generously and completely; but who suddenly, when the hour has come to implement such a disposition, merely "settle down" to marriage in an attitude, as expressed by these words, which might be proper enough with reference to financial status or ownership but is not quite right in the domain of the spirit! For imperceptibly, yet all too quickly, it affects the overall mental and moral tonicity or health of the couple, singly and jointly considered. Their horizons narrow, their contacts with the world of their past experience are virtually cut off: something which is understandable and, as we see it, would imply no detriment if only it were attended by their joint finding of new frontiers. But instead they begin to live for themselves, to shut themselves in a kind of "egotism for two"—later expanded to three or more. They adopt what is wrongly called the "family spirit," which might more accurately be described as a spirit of clannishness or even of caste. Married life comes to be valued only as a "comfortable" reality, whose provisory character they are unwilling to face, and which they take the habit of defending, fiercely if need be, against attacks from the outside. And, too, these young couples begin to practice a "nicely regulated" married life which alternates between material preoccupations, and concern over teaching the children good manners so they will honor their parents; and Sunday Mass which they would not miss for the world because it offers the chance to meet others like themselves and provides a vague sense of insurance against an equally vague "eternal fire." Who can deny that a goodly number of "nice young couples" finish—the word "finish" has been deliberately selected—just that way?

The most terrible thing about all this is that in a sense they are right, because they should indeed shape and guard the conditions that shall give equilibrium to their family and home. But it is all too natural and easy to become so absorbed in this quite necessary task as to lose sight of the fact that it is not, in short, the be-all and end-all of marriage. There is a natural tendency to forget that something or everything might some day turn into an enigma defying solution by any human equation, and that some preparation might be advisable for such a contingency. There is a natural inclination to forget that married life is a kind of training course for another and fuller life which is pitched in a much higher and more vibrant key, and that here really lies the essence of the dynamism and joy of marriage.

The penalty of such forgetful disregard is the inevitable rebirth in the mates of those selfish reflexes against which they had waged such a brave battle in their youth. In the married couple caught under the dead weight of its temporal condition, and bogging down in a dominant concern with this condition, each partner is bound to become ensnared again gradually and unconsciously in a selfishness over which there was never a complete individual victory, and against which there is now no joint striving.

The ideal marriage, reflecting the comprehensive teaching of the Church, is a starting point and not a terminus or a resting place. Wide awake and determined, the partners ought deliberately to set forth on a future course of mutual training with the courage to see beyond the vistas of time while yet encompassing and using time within a sound and sensible range of view of things. It becomes a question of shaping oneself into an offering dedicated to a primal community, the aim of which is dynamic, destined to promote in each of its members the orientation of the self toward complete altruism and toward the entrance through death and the Cross into the Resurrection. It is literally true that no marriage could be truly Christian unless it were visualized and lived out in this perspective.

The child itself through the demands it makes upon the parents should contribute to the development of the higher and longer view of marriage. This ought to be so not only because in its earliest existence the child preoccupies the parents in care, worry and time, but the more so because it is a personal being to whose service the primal conjugal community is of itself ordained. Considerations like this can have far-reaching effects as to how much the child's personality should be respected, and might change a few so-called traditional, authoritarian and glib concepts in education. They could also lead to creating for the parents eventual demands in self-sacrifice of the cruelest kind. For example, what mother can accept clearly and calmly the incalculable consequences of her passing the fifties and to do so without tending in the least to consider her last sixteen-year-old son as just a boy who is escaping from her? This strange young man who blindly and sometimes incoherently demands his own proper and legitimate autonomy reminds her of an inescapable truth—a truth which comes to mind with dreadfully brutal impact unless one has made long preparation to accept it—the truth that the time has come for her to think of old age, and so of death. If I am to believe the lessons of my own dealings with young married couples, rare indeed are the families who are able to absorb without a trauma the impact of this very hard stage in life's conflict. The only palliative to the harshness of such blows is found in lifelong conjugal training in spirituality.

Now marriage, as understood according to the Christian concept of the world itself and of man's destiny, cannot be anything but a temporal reality. We have established that it is the means within the bounds of time on earth for the preparation of humanity's access to the Kingdom of Eternity and, by virtue of its sacramental quality, for the building of the Kingdom of God. Thus marriage is not itself eternal, as can be readily discerned. For if marriage stamped the union of two persons with a mark of eternity, remarriage would be impossible and unthinkable in the event of death striking down one of the mates. This was precisely the objection with which the Sadducees sought to test Christ, though not in an attack on marriage but as an expression of their disbelief in the resurrection. All three synoptic evangelists * tell the same story of Our Lord's availing Himself of His enemies' sarcastic cunning to confound them all with a teaching that opened wide the traditional frames of reference on the subject, with the transcendent logic of mystery.

* Luke 20:27–36; Mark 12:18–25; Matthew 22:23–29.

"For at the resurrection," says Jesus as quoted by Matthew, "they will neither marry nor be given in marriage" (Matthew 22:30). This means that sexuality, which is the specific character of the marital union, will no longer be exercised, precisely because the reproductive function of sex will no longer have reason to exist. It does not mean that persons will not be marked in the most intimate recesses of their psychological being with the characteristic differences of sex. The joy of unity in sexual union will be transcended by the infinitely more direct and total joy of participation in the unity of God Himself. The impermanence of the enjoyment derived from sexual relations arises from the twofold fact that sex is on the one hand a function of reproduction and that, on the other, in the definitive Kingdom of Eternity the sum total of human persons destined to populate the heavenly Jerusalem shall have been attained. Joy then will no longer be derived from a transient union linked with the power to procreate, but from the fullness of reciprocity in the eternal contemplation of the Oneness of God. In this, sexuality as such will no longer have any part to play.

Marriage is in a way an apprenticeship to Divine Love with creative cooperation as the occasion for its practice. If the mates wish to remain consistent in their adherence to the Christian view of human destiny (a view that is founded on the power of the mystery of resurrection), as they showed they wanted to do on the day of their union before the Church, they must be profoundly imbued with the idea of the transience of sexuality as a generative function. It will follow that from the very outset of their marriage they will have reasons to avoid falling prey to the violence of instinct. They will be intensely motivated to seek in their marriage something quite different as its primary value, and hence to engage jointly in practicing a certain asceticism with regard to their sexuality. Keenly and deeply alive to the real significance of their union in the warmth and light of the Charity of the Mystical Body they will find it less difficult to advert to this self-denial, accept its necessity and affirmatively practice it.

The need for an integral view of marriage

Though, as we have pointed out earlier, sexuality and its exercise gives to the conjugal union its specific character, it is not, from the point of view of communality, the goal of marriage. Proof of this can be found in the recognition granted by the Church to unconsummated marriage, the union in which the partners mutually agree not to exercise the sexual function. Such a marriage is a valid contract, provided abstention from intercourse has not been set as a prior condition of the partners' mutual consent to become married; and only the most exceptional reasons justify this kind of union, for procreation is a duty of fruitfulness for two young and healthy persons who unite before God. The only reasons which can take priority over this duty are those of a supernatural or, one might say, of a mystical order.

It nevertheless remains true that the sexual instinct and the function it activates cannot be placed

in the absolute forefront of all conjugal considerations. Both the instinct and the function must be
integrated harmoniously in the comprehensive plan
of married life, related to the common desire of the
mates to prolong themselves in the child, as well as
to participate in perpetuating and extending the
species. Instinct and function in sexual matters rank
as a specific privilege, and must be so placed in the
comprehensive synthesis of the couple's life. Sexual
union must assume for them the character of a
token, a guide mark, a summit in their life in common, a life so close to being oneness that creation
of a new living person is foreseeable and within
range of its realization. However, let it be said
again: sex as a function cannot possibly be dissoci-
ated from the generative power.

In this harmonious synthesis of all personal elements, an integration which represents the whole
life of the couple, it is quite evident that sex, though
it has a quality of supreme intensity, constitutes no
more than a rather short and secondary moment in
the live-long day. Life in common stretches day after
day into areas of activity usually far removed from
anything directly relating to sex, and if the search
for unity were given up or allowed to become hap-
hazard in all these other areas, it would be useless
to look for true and worth-while union on the sexual
plane. Moreover, even if unity were achieved exclusively in sex—a unity which the least pessimistic
observer could describe as a simple synchronizing of
enjoyment—it would amount to bitter illusion. The
mutual and true giving of self goes on all through
the days, all through the minutest details of life together; it does not just happen to occur in the fleet-

ing moment of the sexual act. The gift of self is more exacting in its demands and more difficult to achieve when thus set against the background of daily humdrum existence. It requires on the part of each member of the marital team a constant and methodically deliberate effort to drive oneself beyond one's laggard self; a straining to give for the sake of unity and true balance, really everything one has, not just each individual's sexual potentialities.

The sexual behavior of a married couple, therefore, fits into the synthesis of their general behavior; and this, in turn, can hardly be conceived—at least in a Christian perspective—as anything but the corporate disciplining, training and education of *all* the power of their instinct, of *all* their impulsive dynamisms, of all things, in brief, over which the mind has not as yet achieved sufficient control. Love, in the most spiritual sense of the word, is alone capable of wrenching free these two persons from their congenital selfishness and of setting them on this course of corporate and mutual education. And no instinct can be allowed to be taken out of the curriculum, not the sex instinct any more than the others. Man's ultimate destiny demands that he aim for the highest possible mastery through mind and spirit over the ill-defined and unpremeditated forces of his being or, in other words, that he achieve maximum disentanglement from the tricky snares of mere sensory pleasure and, with greater reason, rank carnality. In wedlock, release of this kind is effected by joint effort, and it is quite normal that the sexual instinct should in this regard be of common concern. Conjugal chastity shall not then primarily consist in *avoiding sin*, but rather in moving together toward a commonly achieved balance and poise which will be an emancipation from instinctive compulsions. Thus set free, man will have clearer insight into the post-temporal world of the resurrection in which, as St. Paul says, the flesh even as to its most hidden impulses will be wholly and sovereignly penetrated with the light of the spirit.

In concrete terms, the ideal couple would be the one in which both spouses had reached such a degree of common balance that in the face of the necessity, for example, of practicing continence over rather long periods both husband and wife would not find it at all difficult to forego intercourse, *precisely on account of love and its demands.* I am thinking here of a couple whose story I was privileged to know: a new birth was out of the question for many long months to come, but the husband as he held his wife in tender embrace, spontaneously and in apparent unawareness of the tremendous implication of his words, said: "I love you too much, even too much to desire you." Apart from their spiritual and religious significance, such words revealed the presence in both persons of a singularly well-balanced condition of emotions and instincts.

Berdyaev's profound observation in his book, *The Destiny of Men,* is in line with this couple's true-to-life intuition: "Genuine love is the most powerful means of rising above sexual lust, the source of downfall and enslavement."

Obviously, for the sake of conforming with an integral view of marriage, sexual union will have to be invested with certain characteristics imparted to it by the actual life experience of the partners.

Though it is commonly said that the question for them is to avoid bogging down in mere search for sensual enjoyment, it is definitely not a question of denying this pleasure, or of considering it evil, or of rejecting it. The real point is that delight of the flesh must serve as a prop for something else, and is not to be sought exclusively for its own sake. Doing so would constitute at least a venial fault, according to the teaching of Pope Innocent XI in 1679, in his condemnation of laxism.

Ideally, sexual intercourse should be viewed graciously, and not under precept, by each partner as a fulfillment of the other partner's well-being for the good of their community. The joy of their union and even its delight should above all consist for one partner in the rebound of the joy and delight experienced by the other, through the complete oneness of the couple. This, it should not be forgotten, must always be in mutual exchange, as the most effective way of checking the human tendency toward self-centeredness.

Moreover, to square with ideal psychological normalcy, sexual intercourse should be viewed only as tied in with the joint procreative powers of the couple. The woman is able readily enough to take this view, but the man must also adopt it, though in slightly different psychological focus and adjustment.

Recapitulation

This then is the ideal integral concept of sexuality in married life which the Church and which Reve-

lation and tradition invite us to consider as our
goal and exemplar. It is out of the question for the
Church to accept any devaluation whatever of a
synthesis which gives to the most natural aspira-
tions of love their ultimate crowning and perfection
from above, while at the same time it sets aside
as fundamental inadequacies all deliberate defaults
or transgressions.

Love means the total mutual gift of self; the
acceptance of the necessity of a corporate asceticism;
the joint training of the sexual instinct and its
orientation toward goals that transcend its own
quality, the refusal to dissociate sex from its reproductive ends; the curbing in each mate of selfish
reflexes even in carnal union. Such are the essential
points of the Church's moral and ideal directive
teaching on marriage as related to humanity's ultimate destiny: the world of the resurrection.

Practical results of the integral viewpoint

Short of self-contradiction the Church is bound
to mark as a fault any infringement of her magnificent ideal. A couple that consents, in common
judgment of values worth seeking, to such infringement is fatally in error, and perhaps in sin, if consent is clear, deliberate, and given in full freedom
of mind and with full knowledge of the facts.

In another connection, since the sexual function
is directly related to love and the generating of life,
it must not be undervalued. For sex indeed commits
man to participate in the most mysterious and greatest dynamism in the whole universe, and it is es-

sential in the highest degree that his participation be flooded to a maximum with the light of conscience and spirit. Moreover, the force of natural attraction and of creative fusion in two persons of complementary sex is appropriated by the sacrament in the act of their mutual consent officially entered into before the Church. In this perspective conjugal love becomes in the proper sense a mystery, that is to say, a reality by which not only divine power but also the grace of eternal salvation will be actuated here on earth. When husband and wife do their utmost to conform with the ideal described by the Church, their harvest is a flowering of eternal values. This is nothing like a mystery in the psychological sense, much less a kind of taboo or setting apart of persons from which something magic is expected to result. It is a religious reality even before it is a moral one, for it is a rite of nature with a biological and emotional significance of natural proportions; but the grace of the sacrament broadens its significance until somehow it concerns even God Himself.

In concluding this chapter, it ought to be noted that we have dwelt on only the *objective* aspect of the question of conjugal morality. In other words, it was a presentation of the *Law*, of the aggregate of norms required by such a concept of sex and marriage as had received its pointing-up through touches of Revelation and Christian tradition.

But it was all theoretic, general, and hence impersonal. What about the *subjective* aspect of the matter, the real condition of people both individually and as couples as they face this ideal pattern of behavior? The ideal is powerfully supported by the natural laws of the universe and by the word of God, enough to elicit firm belief from anyone whose eyes are lighted by faith. But what about man as he is? This is quite another question, and one to which we must now turn our attention.

5

The Concrete Conditions
of Marital Life

IT MUST be readily admitted that mankind in its concrete reality and under factual conditions is too often inadequately prepared to measure up to the coherent, rich and magnificent ideal which the Church, in God's name, proposes for married love. As far as the integration of instinct is concerned, man's emotional complex presents more of a chaos than a living and harmonious order. St. Paul describes concisely in his *Epistle to the Romans* the conflict between the superior faculty of will power and the darker impulses of human nature which so often strain in opposite directions. He states also the deep-seated and mysterious reason for this conflict, but it could not be expected that he would explain its psychological mechanism since Revelation is not concerned with this purely scientific point.

Should it become possible through the advance of scientific studies of man to examine that mechanism at closer range, and to understand better the chainwork of psychological phenomena underlying or perpetuating man's turmoil, it would then be feasible to supply him with purely natural means—like some kind of mental hygiene—to help him conform with the ideal of behavior. In principle, hoping for such a solution is neither madness nor idle pretension. Progress in that direction would not, of course, root out all difficulties within a defined period of time, but at least there could be some easing of the task for those who have by free choice elected to seek to conform with the ideal. Helping such people at the scientific level would consist in slackening certain excessive or misapplied tensions, thereby allowing these willing subjects to apply their efforts in ways more judiciously chosen and better understood.

Now some progress is indeed beginning to show in tangible form. The study of instincts and of the subconscious, and particularly the study of the sexual instinct and its evolution, is contributing very substantial elements of knowledge to modern thought. Credit is due to clinicians like Freud and his successors for having first entered upon such a study and then advancing it to the rank of a well-organized science. For nowadays, man's behavior with all its possible modulations can hardly be the subject of fruitful investigation unless one turns for enlightenment to depth psychology.

The contribution of this new science is evidenced in three stages which are complementary to one another. First, the new technique methodically reveals unconscious emotional substructures upon which our higher psychological life is based. Next, in this discovery are brought to light many psychological mechanisms which account as efficient causes for the conflict mentioned by St. Paul, namely, the frequent contradiction between the higher spiritual will and the disposedness of the emotional will to obey or not. Finally, when the hidden mechanisms have been uncovered, this new science offers full-scale therapy to help in blocking them, at least partially, and in unlimbering to a proportionate degree man's liberty of execution. The resources of this modern therapy are vast, spreading fanlike from the psychoanalytic treatment of neuroses to simple principles of education and to psychological methods of reeducation, of readjustment or of release. While such a thing as complete mental collapse is relatively rare, there is scarcely a human being who does not fall victim to a greater or lesser degree to the previously described turmoil in the forces of instinct. Such a person may derive benefit from a better knowledge of self, not just as to character (a merely descriptive term) but as to the emotional genesis of that character. Clearer insight into his character thus viewed will enable a man to put the resources of his personality in fuller service of goodness, once he has decided in an act of higher volition to do just that.

In other words, problems of practical morality are so closely tied with psychological problems that they cannot be properly handled if no account is taken of the sure findings of present-day functional psychology. Therefore, after we have stressed how coherent the Christian ideal of marriage really is, we must try to acquire at least a general notion of the psychic realities involved in the pursuance of the ideal We will then be able to outline the plan for a practical morality of greater educational value.

The evolutional character of instinct

The psychological genesis of the personality represents a very long and delicate evolution which unfolds between birth and adult age. It is evident that though the psychical life of the young child be very intense, it is in no sense comparable to the psychical life of the man of twenty-five. Even so, there is profound continuity between these two lives: the same first elementary dynamisms, which are life itself, manifest themselves in a different fashion in both periods of life but remain fundamentally the same. At first glance, the only difference consists in the fact that the elementary dynamisms of childhood have advanced into the domain of clear consciousness, and consequently into the domain of liberty. But it is very important that one study closely the passage from unconsciousness to liberty, because it is quite possible that some of the primitive modalities of early psychical life—which one must describe as unconscious—may persist unduly in adult life, putting the brake by their presence or their unaccustomed intensity on the total development of clear and free consciousness.

Speaking in very general terms one could express this passage by analyzing the progression of the vital needs of the person in the course of growth. It is clear that life expresses itself in needs: the need for security, for sensory satisfaction, for expansion and for release of tensions whatever they may be Corresponding to these needs are dynamisms which engage in actions or reactions that are likely to assure the satisfaction of the needs.

At the early stages of psychical life needs are primitive and, if we may use the expression, directly vegetative. The child will insure their satisfaction in a purely instinctive manner. But as the person develops emotionally, then intellectually, these needs, while remaining fundamentally the same—security, satisfaction, expansion, etc.—will be directed to realities progressively more immaterial and less vegetative. These needs, in other words, follow the same progression as the perfecting of cognition: from the immediate and purely sensory knowledge to rational knowledge which permits the apprehending of abstractions and general ideas, and is the exclusive privilege of the human species. This progression, starting no doubt very early, goes on gradually and in almost unbroken continuity. Still it has a few marked stages which the psychologist or the clinician may use as points of reference. Each one of these stages shows that the vital dynamism of the self seeks by virtue of its very nature not only a constant increase in autonomy but also closer adaptation to the outside world in all its forms. These appear to be the two characteristic lines followed by growth in psychical life as it moves, to quote Charles Baudoin, "from instinct to mind."

Analysis seems to indicate that this evolution takes place not because the disappearance of one need causes the person to look for some new and more complex need, but because reflection on new things awakens a strong desire for them and causes the previous need gradually to wane and lapse. The dynamism of self does not stand idle in this slow process which opens doors upon the surrounding world; but for the evolution to take place under the best possible conditions it is indispensable that the needs of earlier stages be properly and adequately satisfied. Otherwise the emotional dynamism will not be totally free to meet the challenge of newer needs, being cramped by some fundamental frustration for which it can no longer compensate. As a concrete example one needs only to consider the stage of weaning: in order for a child to discover the need of autonomy in his feeding and the need of greater independence from its mother, and consequently to be allowed to seek a less passive form of affection, it is prerequisite that the nursing period shall have gone on without too many difficulties, deprivations or distress.

Passing through one stage and on to the next, the conscious self, the real autonomous personality of the subject, must normally reach adult balance. Regardless of the person's intrinsic worth, modalities of action and reaction—the behavior pattern, if you will—must be no longer just instinctive but intelligent and free-willed, definitely conscious and bearing the clear stamp of personal self-determination. In other words, the deep impulses of instinct must be taken up by the higher power of the mind without conflicts of too serious a nature between intellect and instinct.

To describe briefly the essential mark of balance in adult personality, we might say that it consists in the proper socialization of instinctive tendencies. For example, the instinct of aggressiveness that corresponds to the needs of security and expansion and the instinct of pleasure that corresponds to the needs of satisfaction and release are integrated within the subject so as to be oriented no longer just to him but to a community of some kind. The nurseling loves itself instinctively and with no awareness of the ambient world; the child, at an early moment but for a long period of time, tends to love surrounding things in the degree they affect him, and this attitude of his is naturally egocentric; but the completely adult person loves himself, if one may so state it, in a community to which spontaneously and on first impulse he gives himself. This amounts in short to a total reverse shift in the direction of the dynamism of self, a reversal brought about jointly by interior powers of growth working very gradually and by the progressively experienced demands of an outside world. It is a process that can at times be stormy and dramatic, as, for example, in the adolescent stage.

If any instinct calls for "proper socialization," the sexual instinct does. As a force it expresses an essentially relational function, in that it means the integrating of self with another person of complementary sex for the good of the species. This other person must be considered as really other and not as a reflection of one's self; as a term of exchange and not in function of one's selfish needs. For this other person is also a "self" whose own reality demands to be considered in its acknowledged and accepted individuality. Should this consideration be lacking, sexual relationship in the broadest sense would be radically out of tune. The maturing of the adult by dedication of the self to another must, of course, be achieved not only at the intellectual level but also at the level of spontaneous and instinctive disposition: what is required is not a right *notion* about relations between persons, but an attitude of emotional readiness to give one's self, which is a proper overlay for the deepest of instinctive forces.

Finally, the complete perfecting of the growth of sexual instinct demands that both its purely emotional aspect and its neuro-vegetative side—commonly described as the physical side of sex—be dealt with. The rightful consummation of growth to adulthood in sex is manifest when those two elements have been fused in the attitude of giving. In other words, a human adult who has achieved normal maturity should react sexually in spontaneous and intense fashion *only* with the person of opposite sex whom he loves—not just wants—and this out of a spontaneous yet freely willed desire for mutual exchange and unity.

It is easy to realize, now that these points have been made, how long a road the evolution of the sex instinct must yet travel before it reaches this state of perfect balance. Current literature, whether or not it has great literary value, too often attests to this disappointing fact.

6

Difficulties in the Evolution
of the Sexual Instinct

NORMAL EVOLUTION of the ego in all emotional aspects at once is never in fact completely achieved. For human nature is prone as the result of original sin to a certain retardation which beyond any hope of natural, total, and permanent achievement impairs psychic and spiritual development even though moral freedom is not for that reason suppressed except in pathological cases.

Now depth psychology offers the means of analyzing the mechanisms of this stagnation and may perhaps help in circumscribing its damage either by showing how to avoid certain errors in education or by aiding the subject to shake off its extreme effects.

The first force which threatens to hamper the growth of an affective personality if it is constituted poorly or if it functions inadequately is the super-ego. In the child who is confronted with primitive impulses demanding only a free exercise a reflex organism will develop whose aim it will be somehow to regulate such exercise. The child will be submitted to prohibitions, first of the breaking-in variety, then of educational caliber. Some of the "don'ts" will come from living or inanimate things, animals or objects, whose own specific weight or density resists the blind push of the child. But other vetoes are spoken by the proximate human world of the family circle, itself subject to many prejudices of caste, class, race or culture. The child, as yet unable to react, except sentiently and emotionally, takes in these prohibitions at the level of his instinct and appropriates them, as it were, in purely reflex assimilation wherein fear—of insecurity of deprivation—plays a significant part. In very short order the child's psychic make-up is riven by these two opposing forces which are devoid of rationality but are endowed with the spontaneous energy of instinct. In the ensuing inner argument the super-ego is cast as the theoretically regulative counter-impulse, but it is only emotional. In order that an ultimately usable foundation might be laid and that the conscious ego might in the light of the mind work out its rational behavior or morality, every one of the prohibitions which arouse and build up the ego would have to be perfectly fitting, relevant, flexible and consistent with the necessity and objectivity of the real world. Every "don't" should also be carefully shaded lest, for example, a "don't put your finger in your nose" register emotionally with overtones of importance and drama equal to those involved in the command not to take a neighbor's goods. In other words, the only effective checkmate to the super-ego's interference with the ultimate development of self-reliance and good moral behavior would be the existence of a world of paradisiac perfection where kitchen ranges do not burn fingers, cats do not claw, and parents are paragons of composure, poise, understanding, intellectual refinement and self-dedicating love. In actual practice, however, one must be content if the development of the super-ego unfolds without too many emotional setbacks, without too much gross confusedness, and if the super-ego lends itself later to reasonably accurate rough drafts of well integrated behavior.

The second factor which may set in motion the regressive force mentioned above is the sense of frustration, with an attendant reaction of narcissistic turning back to self. In order for the dynamism of the ego to move in unhindered fashion up to the level of higher needs proper satisfaction of primitive and inferior needs must, as we said, have been provided. If this has not happened, the affective personality is left thirsting, as it were, since the subject has a sense of having been denied something to which he was rightfully entitled. This feeling of frustration is not conscious, of course, nor could it possibly be rationalized in a child of one, three or six years of age. It must then be of a reflex nature, as will also be the reaction it will cause. All goes on, then, as if the emotional force turned back in a kind of nostalgia to the past and to itself, seeking somehow to fill an instinctively detected void. The freedom of evolution of the ego is thereby definitely impaired in lesser or greater degree according to the intensity or the importance of the frustration. In extreme cases one may witness behavior patterns like the following in a little five-year-old girl, as reported by Doctor Leuba: "She spends all her time alone, not playing any games, but repeating to herself, 'my poor little duck, it's lucky you have yourself!' "

A child that lacks the warm affection of its parents at the age when the first emotional impulses are felt will begin life under a heavy handicap liable to throw forever out of tune in him the foundation of instinctive forces. This is amply proved by the number of problem children found in homes described as broken—broken by divorce, or lacking stability because of a common-law union. The problem child will always suffer more or less imperative recurrences of primitive needs in symbolic form now singularly ill-adapted to his present life: obsessions, phobias, anguish, nervousness evidenced by nail-biting, etc. What grown man can state objectively and in good conscience that he never suffered any emotional frustration whatever? In the world as it exists and functions, such a claim would be a puerile lapse from truth.

The child's difficulty in moving forward from an early need to a later more complex one is exemplified most strikingly perhaps in the Oedipus conflict. Here we have a little boy who so far has been utterly dependent upon his mother and has demanded in reflex manner her complete dependence on him, all this without the slightest shading. Now as his faculties of perception progressively develop he discovers, still at the level of emotions, of course, that a third party is involved—the father—whose importance he realizes looms large in his mother's emotional life. He feels frustrated; or rather, to put it in more exact terms, if this tense situation is not resolved in him by a positive adjustment of his reaction toward his parents, he runs the chance of feeling denied an exclusive possession to which he believes with every fiber of his body he is entitled. For there is no rationalizing at age four or five.

In order to clear this stage the boy must renounce an emotional mood which has become too passive; he must cease to look upon his mother as an object entirely at his service and to consider her as a person whom he has to win back somehow by following a pattern of behavior like that of his father who seems to have succeeded in this task. Upon reflection one realizes that this youngster is faced with nothing less than his first experiencing of a social reality, and that it requires on his part quite an effort of adaptation in order for him to find emotional security and satisfaction in a new register. If there is the slightest sign of faltering in the unity of the parents, the slightest display of joint selfishness on their part, or the slightest feeling in the child that he is left alone before or during this period, there will be risk of seriously inhibiting a very difficult emotional adjustment, of inflicting upon the child's psychic personality a painful frustration, and of provoking in him a reflex withdrawal into himself which will impair his ultimate affective evolution. That all these dire consequences are not gratuitously invented by theorizing psychologists bent on creating hypotheses is proved by the incredibly high incidence of cases encountered in the practice of normal or abnormal psychology, and involving emotional trauma of a more or less serious nature suffered in this early stage.

Granting that frustration provokes immediate regressive fixation upon an inadequately settled problem of the past, it also originates, again in a reflex manner, a searching for compensation. The small child of three already trained to be clean will show no reluctance, once a little brother or sister comes upon the family scene, to begin again to wet his bed. This performance is proof that he is ready to use any means to recapture the attention of his mother when it has wandered or been drawn to someone or something other than himself. So frequently does this occur that no further insistence is called for.*

But with regard to what we are now discussing, namely, the evolution and development of the sex instinct, the phenomenon of reflex emotional compensation is of highest importance. Genital sensitivity being no doubt of the keenest, the narcissistic withdrawal will tend to take place in this area as the subject tries to compensate for his frustration through some indulgence of the senses that affords a kind of release of his inner tension.

This fact is rarely cause for concern when a child is about five or six years old, and at the age when the child becomes emotionally aware of his sex as distinct from the rest of his bodily person. Infant masturbation, much more common than people think, does not generally show signs of being pathological: compensation is sought rather in more infantile behavior such as thumb sucking, nail biting and bed wetting.

---

* To explain in this way the incontinence of urine, or enuresis, on the basis of experimental observation is not, of course, to exclude other causes of organic or neurological complexion. It merely serves to circumscribe the importance of these other causes, a limitation which the therapist must not fail to take into account.

But as adolescence sets in it is quite another question. After the period between the ages of 8 and 12 roughly, when instinctive impulses have come to some fairly workable agreement with the counter-impulses of the super-ego and a temporary equilibrium has been reached, everything is abruptly called in question by the outburst of puberty: biological and psychic forces strain to overshoot the limits of an existence which until now has been encompassed within infantile purviews.

With the thrust of biological evolution moving it on to a climax, the drama of adolescence—for it is indeed a drama—is characterized by the fact that from each youth on stage is required a departure from the temporary balance established in the age period just ended, a forsaking of an instinctively self-centered way of perceiving the world about, and a readjusting of all emotional reflexes. All this climaxes in the young person's emerging into a new world, unexplored, forbidding, boundless, hostile and often disappointing, a world bristling with strange difficulties which will necessitate untried initiative. The young person is at once driven forward by the natural expansion of personal dynamism which seeks autonomy, and held back by a kind of vague and indefinable sense of anguish in the face of a task of appalling magnitude.

During the course of the period of imbalance, the feeling of frustration is always ready to re-assert itself, the tendency to narcissistic withdrawal lies near the surface, and compensative auto-eroticism of a sexual nature is within call. For the bio-psychological push of growth at the stage of puberty quite suddenly brings the subject to discover how intense sexual pleasure can be. In the first anguish of frustration, therefore, a youth will instinctively and unwittingly tend to seek this solitary gratification which gives him the illusion that his troubles are forgotten and his tension released. But since such conduct seems morally evil or at least vaguely abnormal and shameful, there will arise a kind of giddy sense of guilt akin to a minor phobia which will not simplify the problem.

It is then that pubertal masturbation becomes a habit. And the psychological importance of this phenomenon is so great that we must dwell upon it at some length.

7

Importance of the Adolescent Stage of Sexuality

FROM THE point of view of the evolution of the self, habitual masturbation whether passing and slight or, on the contrary, as deep and lasting as a neurosis constitutes an abnormal narcissistic fixation, regressive in nature and varying in intensity. Aside from its psychological origin as we have just outlined it there are several other possible causes for the habit or, to be more exact, several psychic conditions which often promote its implantation.

Ignorance, the first cause of self-abuse

The first is beyond doubt ignorance. The silence of educators on this subject can hardly be called a proper approach in preparing a youth to cope successfully with this difficult period. No one has in advance supplied the young person with guideposts according to which he might properly dovetail into his existence the many new physical and emotional factors which come to his conscious attention. The odds, therefore, overwhelmingly favor a crudely inadequate adaptation which on his part will be the result of his instinctive reactions or of response to whispered conversations, and he will never be able to integrate his sex impulses. For if an adolescent knows from repeated admonitions that "sins of the flesh" are grievous but has never been made to realize and understand the changes which are about to affect his body and his imagination, he is still very ill-equipped to govern—not repress—the momentary but very commonplace desire for self-abuse. The remissness of parents on this score passes belief, but it takes refuge behind the best of intentions, such as being reluctant to arouse feelings of guilt. Such rationalizing is childish, for guilt-feelings are a part of normal growth, and a child will discover them for himself, but then only in a confusing aura of mystery and obscurity where all his attempts to sort out, organize and clarify what he discovers will be utterly futile. And so in the irresistible urge to find for himself some kind of guide line out of a maze no one has bothered to map for him, a youth will haphazardly stumble anywhere: through medical books, clandestine publications, and in furtive conversations with playmates. Meanwhile the habit has become ingrained without his realizing its momentous significance, and the adolescent has been brought more or less rapidly to the point of wanting to "experiment" in the matter in order to give himself a surer footing on what for him is uncharted and shifting ground. It is at this point that one hears expressed the theory, current even in Christian milieus, that a young person, and especially a boy, should have some pre-marital sex experience so as to avoid acting clumsily with his bride. Interesting as this may sound, it is nonetheless a fallacy also bred of ignorance, for with regard to establishing an ideal balance in man's sexual instinct experiences of this kind are a singularly poor makeshift, since they are only an extension of the habit of self-abuse. The partner in such tests is in fact viewed by instinct as no more than an instrument for self-gratification, despite all the appearances that affection is in full play at the higher register of emotional consciousness. And so to implement such a principle of conduct is to sharpen the cleavage already present in tendency during adolescence between the search for true affection and the cravings of an unnatural sex appetite. It is a highly mistaken way of taking a calculated risk, and leads only to disaster.

Corrective measures against ignorance

The ideal way, on the contrary, is for the young person to have been gradually conditioned from earliest childhood to the normal facts of his sex, so as never to have had the impression that it was all a hush-hush enigma. At the threshold of puberty it is advisable that the young person be given all the basic knowledge likely to help him (or her) consciously assume a positive attitude concerning chastity, and also that self-abuse be singled out as the ever-present threat it actually is for any human being. The adolescent will then be able to nod in recognition at all the successive developments which unfold as he was told they would; he will feel that he is on somewhat surer ground, and will be able, if he so choose, to skirt the quicksands of withdrawal into self that lie along the path of habitual self-abuse. Thus fortified in the fullest possible realization of the physical, emotional and spiritual realities of sex, the adolescent person will be less the victim of that illusory need for pre-marital "practice," and real love will be integrated to the highest possible degree in this person. This means that there will be complete inner freedom to live out the sexual instinct in function of a loved one who either is awaited or has already been taken to heart. At the risk of seeming redundant it must be said in conclusion that no better means than a careful advance plotting of a course has ever been discovered to avoid wandering in any domain.

Fear, the second cause of self-abuse

The second element which militates for the outbreak of habitual self-abuse is fear, which by the way is only an accessory to the first factor, ignorance. Sex education still remains all too often at the level of moralizing without explaining; no precise details are given as to the nature of the sex instinct, how it manifests itself, what its normal reactions are, from what tracks it must be shunted away if its proper destination is to be reached. Therefore, the adolescent is left to his own devices in search of knowledge concerning sex, for it is a theme that is taboo, veiled in an aura of hazy disapprobation regarding bio-psychological realities which are charged with highly emotional meaning.

Such prudish reticence is very damaging in practice because it stems from grave disregard for a psychological truth, namely, that there is no more effective way to impair psychic growth than to bind it tightly to some mysterious fear, in this case a fear more or less concerned with Hell. Recalling the discussion in Chapter V on the chaotic state of man's concrete condition, with particular reference to the inner conflict between the will and the instincts, or St. Paul's "the spirit and the flesh," it is quite clear that before a child reaches manhood, and becomes capable of understanding the high degree of dignity and greatness of sex as it relates to the mysteries of Creation and love, the inner chaos ought to be somehow straightened out. Now it is surely not through a cultivation of fear, especially fear grafted on ignorance, that anyone can hope to make order out of chaos.

For in adolescence fear has a thousand faces, the more forbidding in that they are ill-defined or, more exactly, indefinable at that age. There is the fear of insecurity: the young person is driven by inner urges to break away from the emotional patterns of an earlier age, but the unknown presses down its anguish upon him, and little by little he finds out that the real world is much less idyllic than the world he had dreamed. Consequently he will take refuge in his dreams or resort symbolically to infantile attitudes and reflexes in order to blot out his anguish. As a corollary there arises the fear of woman as she is in reality. In this matter the adolescent would no doubt be very surprised if he were made to see that his fondness for illustrated pornography is correlated to his shyness with women or, conversely, to his rudeness toward them. This is because woman in reality, with emotional qualities so different from his own, frightens him without his realizing that she does. Therefore he seeks compensation for this fear in a contemplation of dream-women of the "cover-girl" type or in the affectation of an attitude of contempt which makes him appear like a precocious and demanding male. In the final analysis and because he has not mastered his inner conflicts, fear drives him to the romantic or the purely sensuous compensations of self-abuse, for such conduct may imply both those aspects.

The findings of modern functional psychology seem more and more to indicate that the fundamental cause of the habit of masturbation lies in the general adolescent attitude of withdrawal upon self or selfishness based on fear which tends to dominate this critical period of life. The habit of self-abuse is a kind of defense mechanism, ill-conceived and inappropriate, for it is an attempt to escape the exigencies of integration as well as a sort of surrender in the face of the efforts at self-denial which are demanded not only by morality but by the very laws of life and growth. It is in this light that self-abuse must be considered if its true nature is to be understood, its far-reaching consequences properly evaluated, and the equilibrium of the human person maintained in the progress of evolution.

Consequences of habitual self-abuse

It is not overpessimistic to say that the consequences of habitual masturbation (even at its ebb) will always remain a serious handicap not only psychologically but also morally.

The habit is first of all a veritable arrest of normal psychological evolution. The deeper it is rooted, the more it will impede in its victim the full attainment of a spontaneous attitude of emotional giving of self. This must be stressed, for there is some confusion in this matter. Of course, if the subject has some positive standards with regard to love, if he consciously tries to practice genuine charity, he can quite well develop an attitude of spontaneous, spiritual and altruistic love. But this is not so at the level of instinctive psychology; reflexes of subconscious and neuro-vegetative nature remain profoundly stamped with the mark of selfishness which the habit of self-abuse has inscribed, one might say, upon the instinctive biological mechanisms. It may well be possible that a person so conditioned will love his wife with very little selfish return upon himself; but independently of his will and even without his being aware of it he will remain deeply concerned with self-gratification whenever he exercises his sex activities, and in spite of himself he will experience marital intercourse as a form of self-abuse somehow made legitimate. The worst thing, however, is that he will not be able to be, nor perhaps even to think of being, on guard against such aberration, marked as he is with the deep scars of adolescent conflicts.

Moreover, the habit of masturbation, especially when it is accompanied by a vague sense of guilt, establishes sexuality within one's psychological complex in truly obsessional guise. A characteristic of adolescence dwells in the fact that the sexual instinct, though far from being the most important instinct despite its strength, does tend at that stage to occupy first place among conscious preoccupations. Again, it appears upon the scene so suddenly and with such a violent opening that it captures all the attention. But normally the quasi-obsessive character of sex, which is the rule at the age of fourteen, fifteen or sixteen, should be progressively attenuated at a pace with the gradual integrating of sexual pleasure with love. Even though man never achieves absolute mastery over his most fundamental reactions in the realm of sex—as in any other—he should nevertheless be able eventually to free himself from the hegemony of any obsessively erotic impulses in his sexual instinct.

Repercussions of the habit of self-abuse on marital life

Some of the most irritating difficulties of married life are often due to certain unhealed emotional scars dating back to a pubertal phase whose evolution was retarded by the habit of masturbation. They are in other words the result of an inordinate continuance of adolescency in instinctive forces— a condition which itself is the direct or indirect sequel of the habit.

The difficulties are encountered first on the occasion of the sexual act itself. It is no exaggeration to say that many conjugal misunderstandings stem from this very fact, either because sexual incompatibility shows lack of harmony in the sex instincts of the partners, or because this incompatibilty itself becomes an obsession which affects every phase of their life in common. Many a so-called "frigid" woman would not be so if her husband's period of puberty had developed and passed normally. Of course, some reservations must be made in this point of view, for the psychology of the female also poses problems in evolution, as we shall see later.

In the exercise of sexual relations with his wife, the man must bear the following in mind: the progressive rhythm of genital reflexes on the woman's part is very different from the sequence of man's reactions, for it proceeds at a slower and more definitely progressive pace, being also more dependent upon psycho-emotional factors. And sometimes, too, the relaxing phase in the woman following climax is more intense, more lasting, as the die-away curve of sexual excitation follows a more gradual decline. Even the normally constituted man must strive to make the rhythm of his own reflexes pick up and follow the beat of the woman's rhythm if he wants to synchronize the climax; that is to say, to achieve proper adjustment for copulation. But for this he must possess the necessary neuro-psychic freedom which will enable him to hold the check-rein firmly on his own erotic instinct lest it run away in violent fashion, and which will make him capable of pliantly awaiting the development of his wife's reflexes. But in a man who has been abnormally conditioned by the habit of self-abuse there exists

a tendency toward precipitate action, for in masturbation the only concern is for personal release, a
concern which gives the subject a bent or disposition to orient everything to self-satisfaction. Such
a man, therefore, will not in the slightest way be
prepared to integrate freely his own sexual behavior
with that of his wife, in spite of his possible true
affection for her. He will go too fast, fumbling those
tactful and delicate gestures which help lull the
stirrings of anxiety or revulsion always present in
the woman, herself not too adequately prepared for
the exercise of the sexual function, however natural
an act it may be. Results may then reach the scope
of real drama. On the woman's part, the excitation
of the early stages will not be resolved in the
climax, and serious consequences of neuro-psychic
unbalance may follow. As for the husband, he is
grieved, filled with self-blame for his inability to
reach unity with his wife at the level of instinct,
a unity he desires with all his heart not only as
to sexual union but in the comprehensive community of their marital life. In a way of speaking,
he is confronted with a kind of neurological impotence.

It is not a digression to refer at this point to the
common fallacy which holds that pre-marital experiences with women will obviate later mistakes.
It is plainly not so, for intercourse with prostitutes
establishes the same pattern of retardation in psychic
evolution as the habit of self-abuse. The reason for
this is simply that here again a young man seeks
nothing except his own pleasure, reducing the
woman concerned to the role of mere instrument.
There may be slightly less danger from this point

of view in "love affairs" involving a certain amount of sentimental affection, but nevertheless it remains true that the proper and complete integration of the sexual instincts and reflexes can be achieved only with the one person to whom the gift of oneself is made completely and irrevocably.

Through passing years, time brings about considerable changes in personality; yet personality remains first and foremost a continuity. It is trite to say that our adult "character" is dependent upon experiences of childhood and adolescence. No doubt, the past is past and often sinks into complete oblivion, but it has done its conditioning, whether or not we are able to recall its workings. It is important that we do not disregard this fact whenever we think of behavior, or discuss morality. But however true it is that we are as adults, consciously or not, the products of our childhood and our youth, and despite the evolutionary continuity of our personality traits, we must never forget that aside from instances of total mental collapse the possibilities of a better evolution are *never* totally ruled out.

It is in this perspective that it was useful to dwell at some length on the consideration of the adolescent phase of life, and on the repercussions it can have in the sphere of instincts. But the emphasis was on the man, and now a few words must be said about the same phase in a woman.

Sex in the adolescent girl

The problem of the emotional reactions of sex in a girl at the stage of adolescence differs somewhat from what we have seen in the case in boys. Up to this point we spoke of self-abuse as the most obvious sign of arrest and retrogression in the evolution of sex instincts. This is more particularly true about the man. Sexuality in the woman is a much more indistinct drive which pervades her entire emotional and physiological being. To express it in a word, one might say that the young man is more specifically erotic in his reactions and reflexes, while the young woman is more generally sexual in hers. This means that her emotional life is not so readily separable from her sexual life in its organic and instinctive aspects. The result is that sexual emotions will have wider repercussions within her than they have in the boy, whether she considers such emotions attractive or turns away from them with revulsion. Erotic experiences will therefore be in her of more grave consequence, leaving as they do a deeper mark upon the whole emotional complex. Another result is the young girl's readiness to transpose sexual self-satisfaction in the stage of puberty to the plane of sentimentality which will find expression in coquettishness, in the need to feel attractive and even seductive, in a certain self-complacency of predominantly emotional nature, tinged, however, with some sensuality. Now the contradiction which appears in the adolescent girl lies in the opposition between her altruistic tendency to give herself and her very selfish need to be alluring. This contradiction is further emphasized in a young woman's search for security, and in her desire to find someone who will be her protector. The consequences of all these self-centered habits which by themselves are more psychological than erotic in the female adolescent will be felt later in the adult woman on the same plane.

However true it may be that difficulties in sexual continence among married couples have their origin in the man more than in the woman, it is true also that woman's sexual desire can sometimes reach the obsessive state if it has been repressed too much, or obscured with adolescent misunderstanding. But such an obsessive condition would be an even greater aberration in a woman than it is in a man.

As a final observation we must take note of a certain emotional element peculiar to the modern world in which we live. It is a sort of subconscious rejection by a woman of her very femininity which she tends to regard as something that makes her inferior. This attitude is quite widespread and is not at all designed to help in the establishment of adult balance in the sex instinct. In serious cases it may create frigidity, as well as a vague disposition toward Lesbian friendships. Even short of becoming pathological it can gravely impair harmony in the sex relationships of the couple and also hinder their joint attempt at mastering the impulses of the sex instinct.

8

Marriage an Education

MARRIAGE IS therefore a way of life which will of itself enable each partner to outgrow the selfish emotional tendencies which marked the stage of puberty. The conditions of marital life do not, however, automatically bring about this growth: it requires the methodical application of personal dynamism aiming at reducing to a minimum the possibilities of a reassertion of instinct as it seeks to adapt itself to new circumstances. It should not be forgotten that these helpful conditions do not of themselves constitute a fundamental solution to the problem since they do not necessarily preclude all possible retrogressions into the self-seeking indulgences of the adolescent period.

Within those limits married life is helpful in many ways in the evolution of the individual beyond the pubertal crisis, provided at least that marriage is contracted at not too early an age. (It would seem that the ideally proper age is 25 for the man, and 22 for the girl.)

First of all, love in the emotional sense of the

word is a new and dynamic reality of such importance that it takes precedence in virtually spontaneous fashion over the ill-regulated demands of eroticism. It is, for example, quite commonplace for a young man of 20 who falls really and deeply in love to experience at once a practically effortless emancipation from a tyrannical habit of masturbation. If such a love is fulfilled in marriage and therein reaches full flowering through the mutuality of knowledge and interchange between persons, it will be for a time of greater or lesser duration endowed with enough strength in itself to assure the growth of the sex instinct. But if a person merely coasts along on the initial thrust of this impulse of love without engaging from the very first the power of some positive effort to rise above himself, the chances are great that when love loses its drive and must be pressed onward, there may reappear some eddies and surges of the old habit of self-erotism. This would prove that everything was not completely settled and that the subject did not put to good use the stimulus of love in achieving adult mastery over instinct and self.

Of further help in married life is the fact that the demands of constant communal living offer each of the spouses the occasion for the elimination of egoism, not alone in matters of sex but in all behavior. The dramatic ambivalence of adolescence—so often persisting more or less in adulthood as a deep and impulsive emotion—comprises on the one hand the need to wrench oneself free from a condition of emotional life and security which was suitable only to a child, and on the other the anguished sense that everything is insecure in a gamble, where the adolescent is staking his whole life. In the unmarried adult emotional security is often made to rest in petty habits, in little ways of thinking, and even in little oddities of conduct to which one clings with incredible tenacity. As the partners in the communal life of marriage have the chance to point them out in each other, these quirks will be brought out in the open and made to reveal the unsuspected strength of inertia involved in their retention. And community living, particularly in marriage, will demand that each mate renounce all such self-centered traits in order to assure each one's instinctive sense of security, this time at the level of the community rather than in terms of self. From the psychological point of view marriage demands a real revolution, or a real "conversion," in the etymological sense; that is to say, a radically new way of feeling, thinking, seeing and acting. Short of this it risks becoming practically unlivable and of being debased to the level of a vulgar social convention. At the inception of married life spontaneous and tender love will make easy the task of self-renunciation, since of itself such an emotion tends naturally to curb erotic reflexes. But life has a dismal daily quality about it and can make short shrift of romance as well as of those idealistic illusions with which every young person of every era is possessed. And again marriage is but an opportunity proffered; it will not prove helpful to the parties concerned unless both the husband and the wife willingly avail themselves of the occasions for self-renunciation in an effort that will not every day be easy nor always sustained by emotional tenderness.

Finally, the social requirements surrounding married life will contribute their help. In the Christian milieu it is taken for granted that marriage is final, allowing of no possibility of breach, save that of death. Anyone who enters into this perspective finds at his service the assistance of a social setup which is sure, at least in design, to lead him away from any tendencies toward the backslidings of self-love and indulgence. The very solemnity of the marriage ceremony with its practical repercussions in organized social life can help him sweep aside the last traces of adolescence, provided, of course, he is psychologically disposed to cooperate in this forward evolution. In this respect the Church, firmly echoing the Gospel demand that "what God has joined, let no man put asunder," shows infinitely more wisdom than do the civil lawmakers who draw a vicious circle when they legalize divorce. Indeed, the moment indissolubility vanishes, pledges can no longer be integral, even though the conscious intent of the parties to the marriage contract may seem to be oriented toward definitiveness. For there always lurks the unavowed notion that a second try could be made, and this obscure mental reservation which no one ventures to probe too closely opens to the deep egocentric reflexes a chaotic and ill-defined field of action. Once divorce is recognized, it inevitably increases in frequency as an emotional and social disease that is self-bred according to a simple law of psychology, for it gives official sanction to a real retarding of the evolution of instinct, and it confirms in adults the adolescent inability to transcend fretful self-centeredness. The repercussions of divorce are far-reaching, particularly in the large number of children of divorced couples who are unbalanced and blocked in their own emotional evolution. This unexpected result of divorce laws is reaching proportions that are near-catastrophic. And yet it seems that public authorities will let many years pass before they begin to be seriously concerned about it.

Short of an exhaustive study, these appear to be the three principal ways in which marriage by its very structure and its basic demands is likely to assist in the development of adult emotional life and in the proper evolution of the sex instinct. But let it be clearly stated once again that these are nothing more than opportunities and mere invitations voiced by the nature of things. These aids can become efficacious and operative only through the assent and methodical effort of both husband and wife.

With regard to the foregoing discussion and in speaking of the behavior of married people or, in other words, of a moral code, one cannot gloss over the facts of clinical experience. All serious statistical studies seem to establish that about 95 per cent of boys are subject in the earlier or the later stages of puberty to a habit of masturbation of variable duration. In terms of psychological dynamism, and with due regard to satisfactory adjustments, this means that not a few men begin their adult existence with inadequately healed scars of adolescent emotional strife. To state the problem differently, a great number of men will be running the chance of encountering serious difficulties in ideally fulfilling their role as husbands in the common search for mastery of sexual relations in marriage. Statistical estimates are much more delicate and difficult to make where a woman is concerned, for reasons previously noted. But to complete the experimental picture of the male it is necessary to point out that of the remaining 5 per cent, 2 per cent are still more gravely repressed than the others. In the present climate of incredible inconsistency in education (one made up of silence and fear), no more than 3 per cent of all boys outgrow the stage of puberty without trouble of this kind. Only that many (or few) will later be able, if so disposed, to initiate a successful and rapid mastery of mind over instinct, with sufficient freedom from any reflexes of selfishness.

Now these findings may seem brutal and darkly pessimistic, but that is not the point at issue. No useful purpose is ever served by the refusal to face difficulties where they exist, or by the silent treatment of man's primary need of salvation. Clinical psychology leaves not the slightest doubt that in the human being there is something incurably broken or undeveloped; that human nature, though of itself and at the root good, has been vitally impaired; that the forces of instinct, again good of themselves, are somehow never quite completely in harmony with the spirit; and finally, that such a state of affairs receives its explanation, insofar as ultimate causes are concerned, only in the mystery of the first fall and original sin. This is a primary and weighty fact of faith which must stand despite the inability of introspection or of modern psychology to give it precise scientific expression, limited as they are to a tabulation of consequences. On the other hand, the spirit of evil knows very well indeed how to exploit this fault of a wounded nature, either by turning the weaknesses of instinct to direct use against the chastity of the spirit or by leading the sinner to despair along the indirect route of obsession about his difficulties.

It is becoming increasingly clear that any moral code which does not take into very realistic account the foregoing evidence will be nothing more than an abstraction, conforming little, if at all, to the demands of the real man, with the doctrines of the Church and with the true optimism of Redemption and Divine Love.

It seems, then, that two errors must be avoided: first, that of surrendering through a disregard or a minimizing of the objective demands of moral law; and second, that of naïvely imagining that the interplay of grace with psychology is by nature bound to achieve here on earth the perfection of eternal life. True though it may be that we are actually redeemed, by virtue of the sacrament of baptism and of our faith in the Lord, it must not be forgotten that for as long as we are pilgrims here on earth, our resurrection is only begun and in a state of germination.

If these two errors are avoided, and if constant heed is given to the disharmony of instinct with spirit and will, as St. Paul realized, there is perhaps some chance for the elaboration of a realistic morality in marriage, one that shall be exacting in principle but compassionate of individual lapses; which shall take proper and orderly account of all elements of the problem, whether they are biological, emotional, spiritual or supernatural, but one that shall not attempt to bypass a central necessity: that of the Cross, victorious over dissolution and death.

9

Outline of a Positive Morality in Marriage

The primacy of love

THE USUAL presentation of Christian morality in marriage seems blunt, and sometimes offensive, because its teaching is confined to mere recall of the great and sacred principles in the abstract without any attempt to prepare the faithful to receive them, understand them or consider them in practical terms as deeply vital and personal norms of conduct. And again, beyond any doubt, these great principles are too often propounded to the people in so concise and compact a manner that all the implications of certain ready-made formulas are not clarified with the explicitness that could make such formulas effective at the spiritual plane.

Strikingly noticeable, where sex is concerned, is the silence surrounding the uniquely central factor of all Christian morality most consonant with the Gospels and tradition. This factor, contrary to the widespread belief of many faithful, is not purity or mastery of self, but charity. Herein, for example,

lies the one real difference—but a tremendous one—
between the morality of the Stoics and that of
Christ.

On three distinct occasions, Jesus presses home
the point that the first and greatest commandment
is love, and that "from it" come the Law and the
Prophets. And St. Thomas, using the terms of phi-
losophy in the expression of even the highest spirituality, will state that charity is the *form* of the
virtues, in somewhat the same sense as when he
declares that the soul is the form of the body. How
far removed this is from the catalogue type of ana-
lytical moralizing which is too often mistaken for
Christian morality!

If we go further into the study of these two
formulas, that of the Gospels and that of Aquinas,
we can say that chastity is the logical consequence
of the demands of love, and that love alone vitalizes
it. Without this, chastity is illusory or at best nothing more than an inadequate natural disposition.
For chastity is important not so much in its efficacy
as a regulating factor as it is in its deep relation to
genuine charity. We shall not betray St. Thomas'
thought, I believe, if we declare that a man who
achieves the practice of chastity without love may
be said to be living the virtue of chastity to a lesser
degree than another who struggles through considerable difficulties, with even occasional lapses, but
who strains his very soul in the effort to practice
chastity out of love for God, and for his wife as a
person.

If it is considered aside from the overall moral
complex as expounded by Aquinas in his *Summa*,
for example, the virtue of chastity presides over the

regulating of the senses by the mind in matters of sex. In this view it is one aspect of the larger cardinal virtue of temperance which regulates the life and activity of all the senses in the aggregate. To put it another way, chastity is the positive dynamism of the mind tending to release the human being progressively from the inevitable threat of sinking into the temporal values of pleasure. Not that these values are evil in themselves; but as with any good thing, if they are unduly magnified and accentuated to the point of drowning out the true spiritual tone of life and destiny, they cease then to be good, not in themselves but because of the false emphasis they receive. Sexual enjoyment, which has positive goodness when in its proper place under the sovereign direction of the mind, may so preempt the psychological and emotional development of a human being that it diverts this person from all effort to rise above things sensory and temporal. Then it becomes by the very fact of its singular intensity and its deep psychological overtones a grave hindrance to the attainment of spirituality which the Christian view of man and the world considers as absolutely essential. The virtue of chastity is nothing else than the sexual aspect of the spiritual dynamism, both natural and supernatural, struggling for progressive escape from materialistic pleasure. It may be declared that a negative concept of chastity even from the simple point of view of temperance would not be strictly and exactly Christian.

But if, going still further, the effort to be spiritual is put back in the only light which gives it its Christian glow, in the light, namely, of charity, then its positive character becomes more salient.

Mastery of self in regard to the facts of sensuality is obviously very useful. But to what end? Shall it be for a certain satisfaction of self? This would be prideful, or something closely akin to vainglory. Shall it be an attempt to conform with some abstract notion of duty? This would be a relapse into a negative and absurd concept, of no interest to man in real life and entirely out of harmony, moreover, with New Testament doctrine, since there the concept of duty is never expressed except it relates directly and immediately with friendship between men and a living person who is God, as may be found in St. John, Chapters 14–18, particularly 14:21; 15:9–10; 15:14–15.

There is a prime necessity: that of really loving oneself in the light of God, which means loving oneself as God conceives us and intends us to be. In the domain of sex there is no possible doubt of such a necessity, for all through the Scriptures enslavement to sexual sensuousness in any form is scored as opposed to God's plan for the world, as is also enslavement to any form of sensory selfishness. One of the first and most enticing ways of submitting to sensuality consists indeed in breaking up the complete unity of sex by wilfully suppressing generative power in order to keep enjoyment of the senses or of some emotional reaction easily mistaken for a certain flowering of mutual affection.

There is yet another necessity, and that is for each, husband and wife, to "love one's neighbor as oneself for the love of God." In marriage this mandate obviously encompasses the domain of sex. Each partner must strive to help the other to rise in spirit above the chaos of sexual instinct inherent in everyone to a more or less turbulent degree. In this perspective an act of birth control is nothing else than a mutual exercise in abandonment of the moral law, and nothing could be more contrary than this to genuine marital love.

Every human being carries within him broad and deep currents of resistance to his spiritual evolution, and these currents originate in a psychological condition whose arrested development allows the persistence of certain uncurbed tendencies toward juvenile self-centeredness. Thus it becomes clear that the practice of virtues can be fruitful, realistic and truly Christian *only* if its pivotal point rests consciously and methodically on charity.

Remote preparation for marriage:
sex education

Marital morality, thus integrated in the organization of spiritual life, comprises a fundamental requirement: each spouse must be made ready and must actively prepare himself (or herself) for the well-balanced exercise of sex in function with communal living. In this respect a study of marital spirituality is excellent of course; but even this is not enough to deal with all the elements of the problem. This is the area to be covered by what is known as sex education.

Both young and older parents will be likely to exclaim, "Yes indeed, but is it not a bit late for us? Sex education cannot provide us with any solution for our immediate difficulties!"

That is quite obvious. Unfortunately, compensating for a long delay in sex education is no easy matter, and latter-day self-denial, even coupled with a belated inquiry into the realities of the sexual instinct, is never quite the substitute for the ideal of long familiarity and enlightenment fostered by progressive coaching in these matters throughout childhood and adolescence. All the more reason then that concern should exist along these lines for the coming generations. The most elementary duty of love on the part of the parents of today is to see that their children who are tomorrow's adults shall be spared the shortcomings and mistakes which always turn out to be grave in this matter. Sexual instinct is too important a psychological reality to be allowed to develop in a penumbra favorable to all kinds of confusion. And of course it seems truly contradictory to demand suddenly of young people a behavior born of perfectly harmonious and finely adjusted understanding in regard to this essential and complex phase of their activity: and this when they have been deprived of proper explanations about it, and when it has been made more difficult for them by the introduction of prudish, puerile and erroneous notions.

Sex education, or in other words the remote preparation for marriage, is a long and exacting task which must be begun very early. It forms an integral part of general education, and its omission seriously impairs the entire process. The child has the *right* to know, and when he asks questions, very early as he often does, he has the *right* to truthful answers. When he is told this or that story of a cabbage patch, a store, or even a hospital, he is made the victim of a deliberate lie in the strictest sense of the word, for his instinct of absolute trust in his parents leaves no room in his mind for any critical evaluation of their statements. And here lies the most delicate problem for those who have assumed the responsibility of bringing into the world this demanding and mysterious person: their concern must be great that the truth to which the child has the right shall be imparted within the scope of his own inquiries and at the level of his capacity to understand. These elements, of course, are variable for each child, and that is why early sex education can be imparted in the ideal sense only by the parents, progressively and in a strictly personal way which is adapted to each particular child. This is an elementary call of duty on the parents, as the Sovereign Pontiff recently restated it.

It may be said that as a general rule *every child* of either sex must know before reaching puberty *everything* about normal sex behavior within the scope of his or her power to understand; for no child must be taken unawares by the sudden and mysterious appearance of normal biological manifestations, but must be enabled to take them in stride, to develop his own personal standards of behavior in conformity with an affirmative and living code of morality.

But it should not be forgotten that clear information about the natural facts of sexuality, indispensable as it may be, is only a minimum requirement. It must be considered as only one phase of a formation involving first the child's emotions, and then his consciousness. Such a formation is alone capable of laying the proper foundation of awareness on which the subject can proceed to build the structure of his own self-determination in sexual behavior. In the truest of senses, sex education ought to be the methodical and progressive development in the child of this enlightened and rational self-determination—a development at once exacting and respectful. It will sometimes imply cruel renunciation on the part of parents when, for example, they must accept the fact that their children have evolved views on sex which are perfectly legitimate, but at great variance with so-called "family" traditions. Is not such renunciation, however, just one of the fundamental demands of charity? Much might be said in a critical vein about a certain form of education, labeled as "traditional" because it has perpetuated from previous eras many prejudices of questionable religious value. In this education great care was exercised to withhold the revelation of certain "things" in the deceptive hope of maintaining over children the influence of an authority which would make them hold to the "straight and narrow path." The obvious failure of this so-called "method" is its own judgment, but one cannot be too stern in condemning it in the face of the disorders, the inner contradictions and the dramatic maladjustments ascribable in great part to its baneful influence.

The responsibility of parents on this point is heavy. The well-balanced development of emotions and character—the constituents in large part of practical moral living—goes hand in hand with the harmonious agreement and the cohesiveness of the parental couple. Indeed, following Freud, depth psychology has established how profoundly the correct development of the sex instinct depends on these parental dispositions. Without a doubt the child, particularly in his early years, is a veritable tyrant about whom every phase of married life must be concerned. This is as it should be, for he did not ask to be born; and this tyranny which is fraught with joy and promise for the future is simply the normal outcome of the love-aspect of sexuality which first brought together the two persons who are the parents.

If the parents are unwilling to outstrip, painfully at times, their tendency toward selfishness or dare not give the right answers to the first questions about the mystery of life, they will be setting the fragile evolution of their child in the midst of every condition likely to compromise seriously his ultimate development into a person of moral and spiritual stature. A realization of this truth by every parent would doubtless be a great step forward in bringing about marital and family relationships and behavior more consonant with the inherent dictates of love.

The morality of "goals" as opposed to a morality of "acts"

Regarding the actual behavior of husband and wife it must be borne in mind that the usual way of teaching "morality in marriage," is through a "morality of acts," which limits itself to being simply a statement of objective values. As such, this approach is indispensable if there is to be any discernment of the nature of things. But by itself it is utterly ineffectual as a means of giving valid inner concentration and strength to a moral *life*. For moral living does not consist essentially in the avoidance of acts shown to be evil; but in the progressive and steadfast settling and following of comprehensive and cohesive tenets of behavior. This might be called a "morality of goals": for while a morality of acts stresses values in the manner of a catalogue, a morality of goals must be viewed as the personal effort to impart to the dynamisms of instinct in sexuality their full meaning and proper place within the framework of a comprehensive spirituality. Individual acts will then serve only as guide marks, and marital morality as an experiment in living will no longer consist in avoiding sinful acts but in working together at the virtue of chastity—a positive force which flows as a direct result from the total pledge of both spouses in charity.

We encounter now an immediate practical conclusion deriving from the foregoing statements of principle. From the very inception of marriage the couple should logically initiate the common education of their instincts toward an effective spiritual development. The sex instinct, in particular, calls for a methodical and conscious effort in training. From the very start, marriage should gravitate toward an individual and a common mastery of sexuality such as would assure maximum response of this vital force to the demands of love and the dictates of the mind. It is in this direction that the couple, without trouble or disturbance, through chastity and not through repression, shall find it possible to achieve the voluntary self-restraint which circumstances might require. Any other course would lead to moral surrender.

This affirmation might at first sight seem paradoxical, and yet it is the logical conclusion of the Christian concept of man and of sex.

Moreover it is in agreement with the data of modern dynamic psychology. For marriage indeed presents the following hazard with regard to the sexual instinct: husband and wife, who have been striving, up to the time of marriage, to keep themselves as individuals, the masters of selfish instinctual tendencies, run the risk of losing contact of these tendencies if the honeymoon is marked merely by uncontrolled self-satisfaction in matters of sex. The husband will find a reactivation of certain patterns of conduct associated with a remote or a recent habit of self-abuse; while the wife, awakened to genital sensuousness, incurs the risk of absorbing this new experience in terms of an adolescent self-centeredness which she has not as yet outgrown. The power of the sex instinct is indeed so great that unless one strives from the very first to bring it under control, it may well gain troublesome ascendancy or even lead to the complete enslavement of the person. At any rate, an inescapable consequence is the raising of a barrier in the uphill path of complete altruism with regard to the mutual gift of self. Furthermore, the illusion of pleasure or of physical compatibility may be of long duration, disguising the deep antagonisms of a twofold self-centeredness which is not liquidated in mutual renunciation. The eventual clearing of this mirage is generally attended by real tragedy.

The teaching of the *Book of Tobias* is characterized by more than just the intent to show clearly the benefits of compliance with the law of Jehovah.

It features an outline of practical morality previously unheralded in Scripture, and it is essentially a lesson on marital behavior considered as a spiritual endeavor.

The demon Asmodeus who kills the seven husbands of Sarah one after the other may well be looked upon as the demon of lust. The husbands, under pretense of marriage, deluded themselves with the mirage of pleasure, which kills love. Indeed the text quite definitely states that "Sarah had found pleasure with none of them." The only way for Sarah and her eighth husband to escape the curse is to heed the suggestion of the Angel, to fulfill what may be described as the ritual he recommends (this ritual is clearly a prefiguration of the sacrament of marriage), and to spend a vigil night of prayer, relating their own oneness as a recently joined couple to the One Lord of Love and Fruitfulness in Israel. And so from the outset the two spouses raise their legitimate and human sensual pleasure to the high level of a spiritualized offering. Such is the full significance of that scriptural marriage night suffused in the light of the prayer whose text rings with eternal grandeur.

In Christian life, the actual sacrament stands ready to give to human love its full and mysterious significance. But it is not the substitute for psychological and moral effort which it will simply make fruitful. The basis of this effort is the systematic determination on the part of husband and wife to outride from the beginning any movements of selfishness and self-seeking carnality which might still be stirring in them. And this decision must be put at once into the concrete form of acts, so that the couple may immediately initiate the joint quest for a versatile mastery of the sex instinct, and avoid falling prey to mere pleasure. For some this will mean postponing for a time their sexual relations, for the sake of asserting with greater awareness their common will for close unity and mutual agreement.

Of course it cannot be suggested that such conduct can have force of law or yet even practical value as a counsel irrespective of persons, for it is up to each one to use whatever means his conscience tells him are best. But there is not the slightest doubt that if ultimate mastery of the sexual instinct is to be attained with some ease, it is indispensable that the partners voluntarily practice from the start and by mutual consent a flexible spacing of intercourse. Whether or not the first embrace is for a time held in abeyance, the Christian couple who wish to follow the example of Tobias and Sarah, and situate sexual behavior against a religious—and not alone a moral—background, must take particular care to place it on a plane higher than that of neurological or emotional demands; they most assuredly must not make it range with biological or hygienic demands, for rating it as such is incorrect; but they must raise it to the level of those higher acts in which there is maximum participation of the mind —that is to say, of intelligence and love.

It is amazing how many women and men there are, deeply Christian in other respects, who are inclined to consider the sex urge as a categorical imperative mandated by some biological organism or other, and who cannot agree that it may readily be overridden with a pliable effort when the joint good of a married couple calls for self-renunciation. This is doubtless one of the consequences of ignorance in matters of sex, an ignorance incredibly deep and wide-spread, strangely compounded of prejudices issuing from equally harmful rigorism or laxism. Clinical inquiries as well as information volunteered by those who seek guidance reveal the striking fact that sexual intercourse in marriage is generally too frequent—particularly at the beginning of married life—and is looked upon as corresponding to an automatic rhythm which too closely resembles routine.

Now, granting that the marital asceticism to be practiced in common from the start of marriage as one of its inner requisites is aimed toward a possibly very distant objective, one must not see in this a reason to neglect its exercise. For any day there may arise concrete difficulties, and there may appear a sharp disparity between the demands of a Christian marriage and the degree of self-control at one's disposal over the sex instinct. Then frequent conflicts will follow, qualms of religious conscience, and even derelictions, all of which might have been at least mitigated, if not avoided, had the couple known from the first how to be realistic, as much from the bio-psychological viewpoint as from that of spirituality and religion.

In the event a couple failed at the inception of marriage to pay sufficient heed to the necessity of such asceticism, its practice may still be initiated at any time. It is quite likely that it will be more arduous inasmuch as habits contracted together have sunk their roots deeper and have resulted in automatic reflexes. Tangible results of the practice of asceticism may therefore be very disappointing to the degree that material and temporal aspects of existence have preoccupied the married couple. This does not make asceticism less necessary or justify the decision to give up its exercise, for what God asks is not the immediate accomplishment of what transcends our power; what He does want from us is a pliant and faithful tendency toward good. As is clearly stated in the Decree of the Council of Trent concerning the necessity of observing the commandments, "God does not command the accomplishment of impossible things; but with regard to what He does command He teaches that we must do the best we can, and that we must ask for the grace to accomplish what is not yet possible; then He will help so that we can." (Council of Trent: Decree on justification, Chap. 11.) Few texts underscore as clearly as does this one the dynamic quality of Christian morality.

Education of love outside sex

What in daily practice should be the concept and organization of conjugal asceticism?

It would be wrong to think that, because the Church places such emphasis on the duties of marriage conjugal asceticism must be concerned first and mainly with sexuality. To adopt such a concept would be a distortion of the problem, as much on the psychological plane as on the moral one. For the altruistic development of mastery over sex must go hand in hand with the balance of all emotions, barring, of course, certain specific neuroses; and the

Lord tells us again and again that the main thing, the essential consideration upon which all else depends, is charity.

Normally, and also ideally, it may be said that the reflex emotional attitude of the spouses must be such that neither of the two could spontaneously think "I" except as immediately synonymous with "we." Tastes, preferences, habits dating back to the time before marriage should not be suppressed, but absorbed into the dominant consciousness of the real and harmonious life of the couple. And this of course must be mutual, for no unilateral sacrifice could be successful here, as daily experience suffices to prove.

But this reflex attitude, for all its spontaneity and for all the ease with which it may be achieved in the first days of marriage, does not become established and constant without the direct, methodical and uninterrupted effort of will power. There is bound to come a moment at which this attitude will falter in some, perhaps, unimportant detail of daily life, but it is then that selfishness can outstrip the altruistic reflex if no precaution has been provided against such a lapse. Although anger, irritation or sulkiness may appear only momentarily, it points a threat at the very center of balance of conjugal life.

Indeed the whole complex of conjugal life, abstracting from matters of sex, is of the utmost importance in the proper regulation of the sexual problems themselves. For love is an attitude which encompasses life in its entirety, and life itself is but a composite of thousands of sundry happenings which put every possible emotional reaction to the test in the crucible of common marital existence. Now sexual life strictly understood occupies no more than a secondary place among the realities of life. If all reliance is placed on it to the practical exclusion of other factors to assure harmony within the domain of marriage, disillusionment of a cruel sort is in the offing. Furthermore, to do so is to evade the far more engrossing but eminently practical problem of the harmonious compatibility of dispositions.

The Christian husband and wife, aware of the psychological realities of their human nature, and also of the transcendent oneness of their union, will with genuine logic give first consideration to this harmonious blending of their dispositions. This will call for a tremendously exacting and constant effort, for a real "conversion," psychologically speaking, of the "I" into the "we," reaching far into the most minute details of humdrum daily living. It is at this seemingly insignificant level of harmony that love dwells, and not at the level of sexual compatibility which is, as previously stated, of secondary importance, despite its emotional intensity. It requires great and true love to give up going to see such or such a movie, or to sacrifice, for the sake of assuring common understanding above all else, this or that legitimate diversion.

The word "legitimate" is used advisedly, for love rests on gratuitousness, not on rights.

To one who knows the ways of love the smallest things can be of greatest account. It may be the smile and the graciousness of the "Good morning!" which the throbs of a headache or the memories of a bad dream might stifle; the timely silencing of a

coarse expletive out of respect for one's mate; the
delicate and trivial gesture of attention whose only
importance lies not in itself, but in its enormous
value as a token of thoughtfulness toward the other.
These small things and others multiplied a hun-
dredfold call for the constant mobilization of the
energies of a sense of offering, alone capable of
weeding out the reflexes of selfishness carried over
with greater or less hardiness from the period of
adolescence. For selfishness clings with the greatest
vigor to such tiny details, by virtue of the illusion
one has that it is rightful to keep as a private preserve of solitude this small and apparently innocu-
ous area of self-satisfaction. This fallacy is subtle
but fundamental; since marriage is of itself a decision no longer to live in voluntary seclusion or in
deliberate withdrawal upon self, the growth of each
partner is in strict dependence upon the oneness of
their community living; any individual severance
from this unity, however momentary and seemingly
fleeting a respite from tension, must be viewed as
an abdication which is bound to retard the growth
of each member of the marital partnership. The
repercussions of this abdication will hammer first
upon their sexuality, driving it back down the slope
of instinctive selfishness.

I recall a conversation on this point with a married man of thirty-five who had come to me to discuss his problems as a Christian concerning birth
control. Our exchange very quickly assumed the
tone of realistic and serene humor which is not
commonly enough applied in this domain of sex.
It soon dawned on me that this model couple, so
concerned over marital morality, was all too tied

down by individual selfish reflexes carried over from an earlier over-protected education. The following part of our dialogue may be significantly cited:

"What is your preference in cheese?"

"Gruyère."

"And your wife's?"

"She prefers Brie!"

"Well now, your matrimonial skies will brighten considerably the day you decide by common consent and for the joy of creating a new climate to give up for good your time-worn habits and . . . both eat Camembert! After that, you can do the same in every instance where you find yourselves locking horns over any personal bias or prepossession, however valid and defensible. When you have done that, come to me again with your worries concerning sexual continence! They will have been singularly dispelled, I assure you."

There also comes to my mind an evening of discussion with several young married couples who were faced with similar problems. These young people were all disposed to accept as obvious and attainable the demands of their Church when these were presented to them as a dynamic compendium of *virtuous daily living*. For they came to realize that when a man and a woman have spent the whole day in the joyful, yet at times arduous, effort to rise above self in the quest of complete agreement and in individual forbearance, they encounter in the evening no insurmountable emotional difficulties in rising above selfish tendencies in the exercise of their sexuality. This is because the only way to solve the problems of sexuality lies in pursuing the affirmative development of a general psychological attitude. Modern psychology holds this to be true, thus strangely cross-checking, though in a different plane, what the Scriptures equivalently teach about Christian charity and virtuousness. The sexual instinct with due reservations made for specific neuroses is bound to become properly integrated if both partners in marriage agree to this pursuit.

In this present day of rediscovery of sexual facts, and with the recall by the Church of the moral demands peculiar to this too-long-forgotten or disregarded point, it is striking to note that the result of what might seem to be a collective obsession with sex is quite simply a boldly underscored restatement of a truth old as the world, namely, that sex is not everything, and that it cannot be considered harmonious unless it goes hand in hand with love, that is to say, with the mutual oblation of the whole personality.

Ogino's "rhythm," and the amplexus reservatus

In considering different methods whose intent is to help assure that marital life remains properly balanced in the moral sense, one must situate them in the perspective which has just been presented. However, some precisions and distinctions are needed.

Ogino's method or, as it is frequently described, "rhythm" is based on a biological law of ovarian functioning. Of itself, and in the sense that sexual intercourse during a period when fertilization is unlikely in no way constitutes an act against nature, this method is not in the least questionable. It is concerned simply with a kind of pause or respite allowed by nature itself under certain conditions of ovarian regularity. Now these conditions are far from being always predeterminable, since the biological laws responsible for this pause in fertility are not as rigorously and universally exact as the laws of physics, for example. The problem, then, involves something broader and higher than isolated sexual acts. If a husband and wife avail themselves of this natural easement only to satisfy their joint self-seeking pleasure or to insure their own tranquillity, they will be acting contrary to the very spirit of marriage and despoiling sexuality of its complete meaning. It is not that the isolated act is a fault; but the spirit in which the act is performed qualifies it morally. But on the other hand should man and wife find themselves at grips with considerable difficulties, and therefore compelled to foresee a long period of self-restraint and abstention, they may well use Ogino's method as a terminal point of appeasement and rest in their effort toward mastery over sex and a higher balance in marital life. It should not, however, be considered as the ersatz of true conjugal living, or as a substitute for the affirmative practice of virtue. Its efficacy in this two-fold respect would be very problematical, as experience has shown.

The same is true with certain differences about the method known as *amplexus reservatus*. Practiced since remotest antiquity, it poses few questions of itself, since it does not seem to warrant condemnation as opposed *per se* to natural law and contrary to the meaning of sexuality. But it is an entirely different question if anyone claims to make it a kind of panacea whose systematic use would eliminate all at once procreation, self-restraint and sin. Viewed in this light, *amplexus reservatus* raises very serious objections of both biological and psychological nature. From a spiritual point of view it might be said to create a fundamental illusion: that of quieting the anxieties of a poorly integrated and more or less obsessive sex urge by imbuing this urge itself with a spurious quality of spirituality. And one may wonder if it is not in just such a delusion that certain couples have found a certain quietude through practice of this method. Several young couples have admitted to me that they abandoned the practice of *amplexus reservatus* after a few months of married life because "all their thoughts centered on that," and it did not seem right for them to make the general equilibrium of their spiritual life dependent upon the practice of such a method. This common-sense reaction is quite possibly a reflection of the deep suspicion with which the Church considers the method of *amplexus reservatus*. And although she has not definitively settled the question, the Church invites us to exercise attentive prudence in order not to be misled by the appeal of a solution which would solve nothing.

The balanced Christian viewpoint

The problem of the sex urge, when all is said and done, is a directly variable dependent of the idea one has of Christian optimism. The exponents of the method of *amplexus reservatus*, be it noted in passing, seem intent on dramatizing their quasi-tragic fear of sin, particularly in terms of its translation into the material order. And again their sense of the dignity of man appears to be violently offended by the idea of a fundamental disorder in human nature and of an impairment of human dynamism, both of which are irremediable within the span of existence here on earth. Finally, it would appear that their envisionment of the mystery of the Cross is distorted, negative, and not at all triumphant as it should be, if it is to conform with the genuine Christian view and with what we can know of the religious attitude of the primitive Church.

For indeed, is not he the true Christian who, far from grieving in the realization of his sinfulness and incurable weakness, makes them the occasion for a deeper penetration through faith and a more actively lived charity, into the very mystery of the sovereign mercy of Redemption? This Christian attitude, far from being a bitter and disheartened pessimism, assumes the qualities of the highest serenity, resting not on human powers alone but on superabundant grace without which, the Gospel tells us, all is lost.

Married life, like any other calling, requires this necessary integration of the Cross. Just to live life in common already demands the constant exercise of abnegation for the sake of a unity which is ever fragile, since it is but a shadow of the substantial unity of total love in the hereafter. Human love can never be consummately and absolutely successful, for man's condition is seriously impaired. It can be no more than an apprenticeship—a privileged one, of course, as forms of human relationship go—to the transcendent love of the Kingdom of Eternity. But it is inevitably doomed to a failure of sorts if only because it must envisage death.

Sex life, therefore, can only bear the stamp of the same necessary limitations. The Gospel teaches us that sex is after all just a temporal means of expression for love which itself is spiritual. Sexuality will no longer have currency, if we may put it thus, after the resurrection of the body. It is therefore plain good logic to avoid being so overtaken by it as to forget or even to disregard the perspectives of supernatural life. With respect to this, ascetic self-restraint and joint mastery of the sex instinct are aspects of "dying with Christ" which St. Paul points out to be the sole condition for Resurrection with Him.

There is, moreover, another aspect of the Cross which is perhaps not quite so often stressed but which is indisputable and not devoid of importance in our present concern. It lies in the acknowledging of one's inherent weakness. There is such satisfaction in claiming for oneself the achievement of strength of character that it is the greatest mortification of pride to be compelled to admit how frail this strength really is; how much it needs at every moment to be reexamined, bolstered, and put back on its feet; how a trifling challenge will send it reeling down, because after all one is not so perfect as one thought! The great dramatist Corneille has one of his heroes proclaim, "I am the master of myself as of a universe!" In the true Christian concept of things, however, man is the master of nothing at all save of his free-willed assent to the Redemption; and it is this which reinstates him in a dignity infinitely greater than the worth he wasted. Failures suffered in the joint attempt to build up to the affirmative virtue of conjugal chastity may even at times lead to a desire for a sort of abandonment of moral values. But this too stems from sinful pride, for even failures can be the source of fruitful humility in those who lay no claims to instantly attained perfection, who do not feel rebellious at falling short of it, but who are serenely obstinate in the faithful pursuit of it. To admit that one is a sinner is really to carry one's cross, without attempting to shun the problem by assuming questionable concern for the so-called dignity of man. And, as St. Paul says, it is precisely when we are conscious of our limitations that we are the strongest, for then nothing blinds us to our radical need of a salvation, and nothing stands in the way of our having recourse to salvation through an unremitting and transcendent renunciation of self.

The sacrament of penance, in the frame of conjugal life, seems to have as its primary effect the deepening of this fruitful, serene and affirmative sense of humility. It should not, however, be the occasion for dramatizing the problems of sex, nor should it foster the tendency to center one's attention solely upon them. Confession must lead to a harmonious smoothing out of moral preoccupations, to a deepening of humility and to a relaxation of tensions. It is in these ways that the sacrament of penance can most help Christian husbands and wives who have faithful recourse to its sacramental mercy to proceed steadfastly—at the rate best and singularly suited to them and not in compliance with some abstract and theoretic outline—toward establishing in themselves the virtue of chastity, which is to say the mastery over sensuality.

Correlatively with these comments and to do away with all equivocation, it is perhaps good to recall that sex is not love but a privileged manner of living it in the exercise of a potential which is of its nature generative of new life. The sexual act of a couple married before God is not for all its true greatness a sacramental act but a proof, a testimony of love; and its value remains of itself in the natural plane. To devaluate marriage, as is currently done in some forms of education by way of a reaction to an extreme attitude of spirituality previously broached, could lead to the opposite excess of materializing it too much and would be just as inaccurate a view. Common sense steers a middle course between condemning the sex urge as carnal and glorifying it as spiritual.

When husband and wife are out of step

When a husband and wife move together in psychological and spiritual unison, their difficulties are attenuated and may even become a kind of stimulus, if they are skillfully handled, for they are jointly taken over as a common responsibility. But everything becomes very complicated when the two partners are out of step and one lags behind the other. Such is rather more frequently the situation.

Consider the case of the deeply Christian woman married to a man of perhaps great human talent but for whom the horizons of supernatural existence encompass no more than a perfunctory attendance at

Sunday Mass when he has nothing more important to do; and who, even when he does go to church, engages only in a sort of formalism akin to fetishism. Surely this good man will have no understanding of the Church's demands in matters of sex and it annoys him in a way, for he is seriously handicapped with old habits of auto-erotism. Being none too concerned with metaphysics or theology he sees no reason for ascetic self-restraint in an area about which he knows next to nothing in even the most elementary terms of biology or psychology. He goes no further than the fringes of a certain vaguely conscious emotionalism which is bolstered by a few prejudices well-rooted in his interior sense of comfort.

What should be his wife's attitude? To this problem there is no easy solution. If she passively lends herself to her husband's contraceptive practices, she is obviously an accomplice in a sense. But if she obstinately demurs, or if—and this is worse—she evinces the tractability of a victim to a holocaust, she is quite likely to jeopardize fundamentally the unity of the home and therefore also the material, psychological, and even the spiritual security of her children.

Here again the approach to the problem should not be in the direction of sexuality. In her steadfast concern for a more spiritual mind in her partner, the woman must work out in action and not in sermonizing the proof that Christianity is infinitely more than just a Sunday formality, that it consists in transforming life into a constant and joyously serene pursuit of love through self-oblation, and gives abnegation and self-sacrifice an aura of transcendent beauty. Then at the right moment she can broach the question of sex in the same light, evincing a concern not moralistic but truly religious. It is her woman's role to lead her husband to the discovery of the world of grace and of sin and of salvation, bringing to her support in that effort all the resources of charm, shrewdness, patience and intuition with which God has endowed her as a woman.

In the event that the situation is reversed, and it is the wife who shows lack of perception in regard to conjugal asceticism, the husband should proceed in a similar manner, calling upon his powers of persuasion and upon his natural authority. Let him remember, however, that he will achieve nothing unless he ceases being the egotist who refuses to listen to anything, or who conversely never utters a word of protest because he wants "peace and quiet." Daily tenderness, faithful and attentive love at every passing moment of married life will eventually win out even over the incredible hardness of heart of a self-centered woman.

It must not be forgotten that sex, though it is in principle the most effective bond of love, is also and too often the ultimate sanctuary of selfishness, and thus most insidiously thwarts genuine love. True, it must be heeded in the construction of a conjugal morality, but it must not obstinately be made the sole foundation upon which to rest the balanced structure of a life of mutual offering, for married life goes far beyond mere sexuality.

Confession

It is quite evident that the role of the confessor is extremely delicate in these matters of conjugal morality.

As minister of the Church he must restate the dictates of the Christian concept of marriage without any curtailment or omission. Face to face with a person who comes asking for the grace of forgiveness, he is fully aware of the complexity of the problem and of the diversity of personal situations in regard to those demands. If he is rigoristic and abstruse, he fosters discouragement and utterly fails —in human terms, at least—to give aid and enlightenment as requested; if a laxist, or too concerned with allaying apprehensions which might be productive of good, so long as they do not reach the proportions of anguish, he again falls short of being helpful. If he play the authoritarian, over-anxious to wield control over the intimate life of couples whom he directs, he rides rough-shod over free will and promotes the tendency to religious infantilism, all too prevalent in our day. And if discretion and circumspection seal his lips any time someone discusses such questions with him, he evidently can shed no light on them. Married people must realize how difficult it is for any priest, a human being, after all, with his own inadequacies, to exercise the qualities of discretion, understanding, firmness, leniency, forcefulness in guidance, all of which might be considered necessary in unison. Let not those of the laity be scandalized, and above all let them not from the lack of understanding in one

confessor infer that the Church is uncomprehend-
ing, as they might be tempted to conclude, when
they sometimes come before a priest who does not
possess all those qualifications. The value of the
sacrament he administers in God's name is not
fundamentally altered for that.

Here indeed we are moving in the essentially mysterious plane of grace. It would not do to label grace
as a temporal medicament whose prime purpose is
the cure of disorder in the balance of man's instinctive urges. Certainly grace works results which are
perceptible in the realm of psychology, but its effects there are gradual because they are the side
effects of a direct increase in faith and charity. They
become manifest in the progressively clearer sense
one acquires of being part of a humanity saved in
Christ, and proceeding through death to the resurrection. This consciousness gives an ever-broaden-
ing outlook on this world and on ourselves, and the
particular grace of the sacrament of marriage consists in integrating the entire scale of human love
with this outlook. The mere receiving of this sacramental grace will not, of course, change the nervous and emotional reflexes of the recipients, but it
is bound to make fruitful at a higher plane everything they do to adjust to the transcendent view
they will henceforth have of their life together.

Even failures and lapses may then be the means
used by the Holy Spirit to bring about some particular good, as the specific grace of the sacrament
of penance becomes operative in helping each one
to realize more clearly his situation as a fallen creature, not with despair and dismay but in the strange
joy of Holy Saturday's liturgical chant; the joy of

having been saved, the joy of God's plan of Redemption. And once again even one's disenchantment with this or that particular minister of the sacrament can drive home more deeply the fact that the Church is not of human making, and that its power to save souls infinitely transcends the sometimes limited natural capabilities of its members.